ROAR
LIKE A
LION

First published in the United Kingdom by David Fickling Books,
31 Beaumont Street, Oxford OX1 2NP.
www.davidficklingbooks.com

Library of Congress Cataloging-in-Publication Data available

ISBN 978-1-338-80218-4

10 9 8 7 6 5 4 3 2 1   22 23 24 25 26

Printed in China   62
First US edition, November 2022
Book design by Sarah Darby and Keirsten Geise

ROAR
LIKE A
LION

How animals can help **you** be your best self

CARLIE SOROSIAK

ILLUSTRATED BY
Katie Walker

d b
FICKLING
David Fickling Books

FOR JAGO,
A GOOD HUMAN.

—CARLIE SOROSIAK

FOR PENNY, THE WALKER
FAMILY, AND JAKE.

—KATIE WALKER

CONTENTS

Follow the
PAWPRINTS

As a kid, I was always jealous of people in fairy tales. They got to hear the sly talk of wolves, the gentle chatter of frogs, the fast-paced wit of donkeys. I was absolutely convinced that if animals could speak in real life, they'd have so much to say. I'm still convinced. The only difference is, I know now: Animals *are* speaking to us. The courageous hedgehog, the resilient panda, the optimistic caribou – every animal is open about its gifts and lessons.

This book explains how we might listen.

And *why* we might listen.

BECAUSE SOME DAYS,
BEING A HUMAN IS
INCREDIBLY HARD.

If you're reading this book, then you are *probably* a human. (Wombats and moles, for instance, cannot read. Or if they can, they are spectacularly good at hiding it!) So, let's assume that you're a person – and that you worry a lot. Humans are expert worriers. We're constantly wondering what other people think of us. We're always telling ourselves that we're not good enough, that other humans are doing much, much better. It can really make you feel like a squirrel's skittering around inside your stomach.

With any luck, the animals in this book will help you realize:

YOU ARE AMAZING.
You are capable.
And you don't need to be
so hard on yourself.

Here you'll find advice from some of the wisest creatures on Earth. Dogs who exhibit mindfulness. Orcas who keep swimming, despite difficult circumstances. Penguins who refuse to care about what other penguins or zookeepers might think. Each animal will illustrate how it thrives, offering a model of how you might choose to thrive, too. **Embrace your differences, says the platypus. Use your spikes sparingly, says the hedgehog.**

Perhaps you aren't accustomed to learning from a chimpanzee. Perhaps you don't seek out pigeons after a particularly rough day. But truly, animals are uniquely suited to guide us.

Here's why.

We're not so different from our animal friends.

In many ways, humans are a unique species. (We are, for example, rather fond of television. And you'll never catch a dolphin wearing pants and a sweatshirt.) Yet, in most ways that count, we're quite similar to the forest dwellers and ocean swimmers. We're part of the animal kingdom, after all! We dream like cats, grieve like whales, bond like barn owls. Every one of us is filled with expectations and hopes and fears. When you're reading this book, maybe you'll even start to hear the animal inside yourself. It grows louder the longer we listen.

Animals are tremendously wonderful at being themselves.

Every single species in this book has existed for thousands upon thousands of years – through bright days and not-so-bright days. They've weathered storms. They've endured. One of the reasons that they're still walking, trotting, and flying across the earth is simple: They are exceptional at surviving exactly as they are.

And finally, a zebra isn't going to judge you.

Neither will a tree frog. Or a koala. Or a capybara. Animals don't even judge one another. So, let the honeybee show you how it celebrates its individuality. Let the crow caw about its confidence. Let every animal in this book offer advice on how you might become your kindest, bravest, happiest, *best* self.

Follow the pawprints and the flipper marks in the sand.

They're waiting for you.

CHAPTER 1

BEE YOURSELF

CELEBRATE ALL THE THINGS THAT MAKE YOU, YOU!

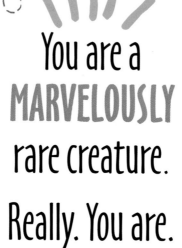

You are a
MARVELOUSLY
rare creature.

Really. You are.

No one else in the world – in the entire animal kingdom – possesses your mixture of intelligence, creativity, and *you-ness*. That's something to celebrate.

YOU'RE UNIQUE!

You're the one and only you!

So . . . why aren't we all shouting that from the rooftops? Why is it so unbelievably challenging to be ourselves?

Well, as humans, we don't always *believe* that we're special. We don't always seek out the things that make us happy. And we often convince ourselves that, to fit in, we have to shy away from our differences – that we must talk a certain way, act a certain way, *think* a certain way.

Kind of silly, isn't it?

It's like telling a hawk that it needs to be a pigeon.

Or a cow that it should be a horse.

When we start acting more like other people and less like ourselves, it hurts us. Actually hurts us. Research shows that authenticity – being your truest self – is a big key to happiness.

➡ **Animals can help us here.**

Animals are _always_ their truest selves.

In this chapter, you'll meet a variety of creatures that offer advice on embracing your creativity, your strangeness, your unique way of viewing the world. Perhaps they'll persuade you to start celebrating yourself as an individual.

JUST WATCH OUT FOR THE RIVER OTTERS. THEY BITE.

Just one of the **CROWD**

So, if you're the one and only you, then why does it sometimes feel as if you're blending in? Look at pigeons in the park: a huge, gray sea of them, nearly indistinguishable from one another. Have you ever glanced at them and thought, *I'm quite a lot like that! Not in the feathery way. But I am just one person in a large flock of humans, and it's impossible to stand out.* You may even think: *There's nothing special about me.*

This is where a pigeon wobbles in to *coo* at you. It's a very loud coo, because he's trying to shout, *Human, you've got it wrong about us!* We may assume that all pigeons are basically the same, but really, **EACH ONE IS AN EXTRAORDINARY INDIVIDUAL**.

ONE BRAVE BIRD ➡

In World War I, a pigeon named Cher Ami delivered a message that saved two hundred soldiers. The enemy had encircled a French battalion — and everything was looking terribly grim. The humans had only one hope left: the shiny silver bird called Cher Ami. She carried a note strapped to her leg, letting the Allied troops know: "WE'RE HERE AND WE'RE TRAPPED!" Cher Ami suffered multiple injuries during her flight, but still managed — with her extraordinary sense of direction and unmatched bravery — to accomplish her mission. The Allies read the plea for help and rushed in to rescue the battalion.

THE ART CRITICS

One Japanese experiment asked individual pigeons: *Is this a Picasso painting? Or a Monet painting?* The pigeons learned to tell the difference! What's more, researchers brought in paintings from a local primary school and asked a different set of birds: *Which are the "good" paintings?* These smart pigeons were twice as likely to pick a painting that showed attention to texture, composition, and detail. Bet you didn't think that an individual pigeon in the park could do that!

DOCTOR PIGEON

In California, several pigeons showed researchers: *We can basically do the work of doctors!* (In one area, at least!) Given a scan of two growths — one cancerous, one benign — these smart birds can say: *That's the bad one. Can I please have my treat?*

You see, other people have so many impressions about us – what we can and cannot do, who we are and who we should be. Quite often, those impressions relate very little to our actual abilities. They say much more about the people who judge us. So, next time you see a flock of pigeons, remember that each bird has a story.

EVERYONE HAS A STORY. YOU'RE MORE THAN JUST PART OF THE FLOCK.

Embrace your **DIFFERENCES.**

Sometimes you might feel a little bit out of place in the world. You might feel odd or strange – like you don't *fit*. During those times, take a good look at the **PLATYPUS**.

WHAT'S THE FIRST THING YOU NOTICE ABOUT THIS ANIMAL?

Or maybe it's the large, **venomous spur** on its back foot?

The **duck-like** bill?

The **frog-like** webbing between its toes?

In the eighteenth century, European explorers landed on the island of Tasmania. When they discovered the platypus, waddling along the riverbanks, they declared it "strange" – so extraordinarily weird-looking that they didn't even believe it was real. "You can't have a mammal that lays eggs like a bird!" they said.

But the platypus has existed – virtually unchanged – since the time of the dinosaurs. It knows a thing or two about survival. Who's to say that it wasn't examining those humans (with their pointy noses, their stubby tongues) and wondering, "How do they think they're going to survive with *those*?"

Humans have a terrible habit of labeling things "weird" when we don't understand them. Maybe your family speaks a variety of languages. Maybe you dress in brightly colored fabrics. Maybe you practice a religion that's different from many of your friends. Some people might witness any of these and say, "Oh, that's odd."

BUT DIFFERENCES CAN BE THE VERY THINGS THAT SHAPE US INTO THE STRONG, REMARKABLE PEOPLE WE ARE.

That's certainly true for the platypus. Its "strange" webbing, for example? That helps the platypus swish through the chilly rivers of Tasmania. The venomous spur? It loudly tells intruders:

STAY BACK!

And that "odd" bill can sense electromagnetic waves from prey; this intelligent mammal can literally hunt with its eyes closed.

Sometimes being an individual means looking, thinking, and acting differently from your peers. And that's *good*. Platypuses embrace who they are, because who they are has allowed them to thrive for 120 million years. **IF A PLATYPUS CAN CELEBRATE ITS INDIVIDUALITY** – poisonous barbs, frog feet, and all –

THEN YOU CAN, TOO.

It's fine to do things
YOUR OWN WAY

Just as animals come in all shapes and sizes, differences do, too. We might look different from others, like the duck-billed platypus – or we might behave in a completely individual way, setting us apart from our friends, our classmates, and even our families. Maybe you like to dance alone in your room. Or create original recipes in your kitchen. Or burst into song in public places, no matter who's listening.

THAT'S MORE THAN OK.
IN FACT, IT'S WONDERFUL!

These animals are going to show you why.

BEWARE! OTTERS APPROACHING!

Don't let their cuddly appearances fool you. Strong-jawed and sharp-toothed, sea otters and their river-otter cousins offer a fierce bite. But their greatest asset isn't their chomp. **IT'S HOW THEY'VE COME UP WITH NEW, BRILLIANT IDEAS AS THEY'VE EVOLVED** – ideas that only otters could develop.

OTTER RAFTS

In the wild, otters often "hold hands" when they sleep. That way, when they wake up, they're still together — and not drifting farther and farther, alone, out to sea.

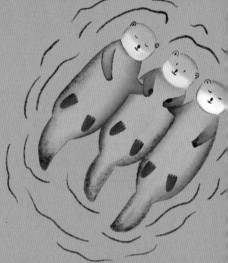

SEAWEED WRAPS

Baby sea otters have the thickest fur of any animal on the planet, about one thousand times denser than the hair on your head. (Imagine brushing that every day!) Their coats are designed for flotation, as young otter pups aren't the most accomplished swimmers. The problem is, while the mother otter hunts, her baby is at risk of floating away. Not to worry! She simply wraps her baby in seaweed, like a water-weasel burrito. There he'll float, anchored to the seabed: content, cozy, and in place.

ROCK TOOLS

SMASH! THWACK! Those are the sounds of an otter cracking open a clamshell, serving herself a nice briny breakfast. An otter will place the shell on her chest and bang it open with a rock — *once, twice, score!* Not even supersmart dolphins use stone tools! Otters are the *only* marine mammals to do so. When they find a rock they're particularly fond of, they stuff it in their pockets. Yes, otters have pockets! Little flaps of skin under their otter-y armpits, where they can store goodies for later.

Otters aren't the only animals who do things their own way.

Bring in the **TRASH PANDAS**!

Yes, I said it. "Trash pandas." It's the internet's nickname for raccoons – fluffy, masked creatures who root through North American garbage at night, scoping out the latest treats.

Week-old bagel? *Yum!* Sticky fruit at the bottom of the garbage can? *Is there anything better?* What they're known for (besides their thievery) is their curiosity. They're puzzlers. They love to solve things: the mystery of how to open a refrigerator, a jar, a Tupperware container. Not every animal wants to explore objects like this. It's rare for grown-up animals to investigate everything from kitchens to campsites with such glee. And yet, every raccoon is uniquely inquisitive, with curious little hands asking questions about its environment. **What does this do? And this?** With almost every movement, with every probing look, raccoons tell us exactly who they are.

Finally, there's Sphen and Magic.

Aren't they adorable? While living at the Sea Life Sydney Aquarium, this pair of male gentoo penguins captured the hearts of Australians when they decided to raise a chick together, even though same-sex penguin couples are a little less common. The helpful staff at the aquarium procured a fake (or "dummy") egg, and both penguins took turns sitting on the nest. The pair were so remarkably watchful, the staff even gave them a real egg to nurture. Simply by remaining true to their own feelings, Sphen and Magic showed how – despite others' expectations – **YOU CAN WALK (OR WADDLE!) YOUR OWN PATH.**

Let's put this all together. In the animal kingdom, it's totally fine not to behave like everyone else. Otters owe many of their survival techniques to trying new things. Raccoons wouldn't have so many tasty nibbles without their curiosity. Sphen and Magic bonded because they listened to their hearts – without worrying about what other penguins or the zookeepers might think.

BE CURIOUS
BE INNOVATIVE
BE YOURSELF

If you're worried that the way you act isn't quite like everyone else, think of these animals – who are distinctive, diverse, and more than OK with themselves.

Find the things that make you HAPPY

Now, we know that you're the one and only you – that you can look, think, and act individually. But do you ever get the feeling that you're supposed to like the things that other people like? In the past couple of months, **HAVE YOU STOPPED TO CONSIDER WHAT MAKES YOU HAPPY? TRULY, SIMPLY HAPPY?**

MEET CONGO.

He was an artist in the 1950s — and we're going to watch him work.

IT'S FUN!

Watch as he carefully chooses his paint colors: **YELLOW**, now **GREEN**, now **RED**. Watch the way he fans the paintbrush across a piece of clean, white paper. *Hmmm, what's it missing?* More colors. More yellow, more red. He's concentrating intensely. After a moment, Congo leans back, admires his creation, and then asks for a new canvas. For him, this isn't just "work" – it's creative expression.

You might have heard that chimpanzees are absolutely brilliant – that they can use tools, form complex social groups, and practice human sign language. But Congo would probably want to stress, above all else, that chimpanzees are individuals. Just as you have a unique personality, so does each and every chimpanzee. Some are timid. Some are more outgoing. And some create artwork that later sells for $25,000 at auction!

ONLY CONGO COULD PAINT AS CONGO DID. That's part of what made him so famous: his abstract patterns, his cleverness. Legendary artists like Pablo Picasso and Joan Miró even became fans of his work – and many, many people became fans of Congo himself. How could you not? Through his 400 paintings, he was tapping into something deep and important: the absolute joy of celebrating his creativity. Of celebrating the remarkable ideas swirling inside his head.

 NO ONE TOLD CONGO WHAT TO PAINT.

NO ONE TOLD HIM: USE THESE COLORS AND THESE THEMES.

What's more, if someone had, he probably would have ignored them, or said: *Go away, I'm busy baring my soul.* He painted for the love of it. He didn't think, *I must be more like this human artist. Or that human artist.* Those magnificent patterns of his? They were *his.* His ideas, his creativity, his heart.

He'd found the thing that made him

truly happy.

WHAT ELSE BRINGS ANIMALS JOY?

Otters are fond of juggling! And trust me, it's otter-ly adorable. They'll flip rocks from one paw to the other, over and over again. It's not quite juggling like we imagine it (otters aren't clowns, after all!), but it serves a purpose. At first, scientists thought these water weasels were probably flipping rocks to improve their coordination. That might be partly true. But one of the current theories is: They just really enjoy it!

There's a softer side to crocodiles. Like many of us, they appreciate a good piggyback ride and love chasing inflatable balls around the water, popping them with their teeth. (Oh, you don't pop beach balls with your teeth? Then I guess it's just crocodiles!) They like to carry flowers between their choppers, too — and blow bubbles in the river.

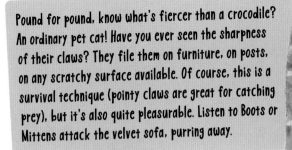

Pound for pound, know what's fiercer than a crocodile? An ordinary pet cat! Have you ever seen the sharpness of their claws? They file them on furniture, on posts, on any scratchy surface available. Of course, this is a survival technique (pointy claws are great for catching prey), but it's also quite pleasurable. Listen to Boots or Mittens attack the velvet sofa, purring away.

Even Pacific salmon — yes, salmon — know how to have a good time. Those elegant leaps into the air? Researchers say, "Yep, some of those are play jumps." Perhaps these silvery fish find fun in the splash, in the way their shiny bodies twist and turn against the sunlight. If fish could speak like us, maybe they'd be shouting, **Wheeeee!**

So, what makes you extremely happy? I bet it's something that comes from the core of you – like dancing or writing or singing. I bet it's something that no one has forced you to like. You love it because that voice – the animal inside you – says, *Yes, yes, this is fun*.

HOLD ON TO THAT.
HOLD ON TO THAT FEELING AS TIGHTLY AS YOU CAN.

It's part of what makes you so special, so yourself.

You don't have to **BEE** just one thing

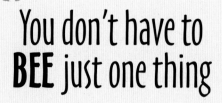

Once you've accepted that you're not just one of the flock – that you're an individual who can seek out the things you love – then another worry might arise. *What if I have to step into a particular role? I said I love football! So, am I just "The Sporty One" from now on?*

At school, do others label you? Do you label yourself? Are you "The Bookish One"? "The Chatty One"? "The One Who's Always Getting into Trouble"?

Well, let me reassure you: **NO ONE IS JUST ONE THING.**

↳ NOT EVEN A BEE

That might seem confusing at first. After all, inside a beehive, it's a symphony of buzzing and movement and sound – and each bee plays a part. Ever heard of a worker bee? A drone? A forager? Those are roles within a hive. And most people only see that label, that one thing.

Over the past few years, though, it's becoming increasingly obvious that bees display individual traits and behaviors – even beyond their function in the hive. Some are more optimistic. Some are more pessimistic. Others are more prone to anger, to forgiveness.

THERE'S ALSO THE WAGGLE DANCE.

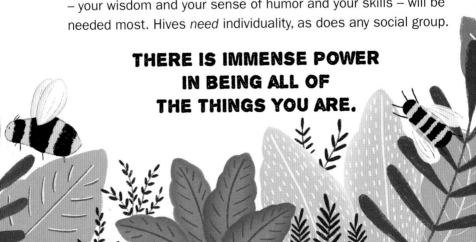

WE LOVE WAGGLE DANCING

I know, I know. That sounds very much like an embarrassing dance your uncle might do at a family barbecue, but it's actually unique to bees. When a forager bee leaves the hive, it searches for pollen and nectar – for food. Oh, yay, it's found some! Upon its return, this bee will perform an intricate, mathematical dance – buzzing around in a precise pattern – that demonstrates the distance and direction of the food source. If you were to diagram the dance, it would look a little bit like the outline of an apple.

One bee does this at a time.
One bee, performing in
front of the others.
Leading the others.

Of course, different bees take turns with the dance (it's not always the same bee waggling! I imagine that would get very tiring), but this just goes to show: You won't always be in the spotlight. Yet, there will absolutely come a time when your talents – your wisdom and your sense of humor and your skills – will be needed most. Hives *need* individuality, as does any social group.

THERE IS IMMENSE POWER IN BEING ALL OF THE THINGS YOU ARE.

REMEMBER
THAT NATURE FUNCTIONS
BEST WITH
DIVERSITY.

Forests only thrive with a variety of trees.
Oceans only flourish with a mixture of fish.

The world, quite literally, needs your individuality.

It needs you to be confident in who you are.

CHAPTER 2

ROAR WITH PRIDE

FIND YOUR
INNER CONFIDENCE

The human world can be **super intimidating**. Sometimes, when you walk into a room of strangers – or even a room of friends – your heart might start pounding. Your palms might start sweating. When you're standing at the edge of a swimming pool's high-dive, or placing your hands on a piano's keys, just before a difficult song, a thought might scramble in, like a particularly frantic squirrel:

Oh gosh, what if I fail? What if I'm **NOT GOOD ENOUGH** after all?

Animals have that "oh gosh" moment, too. They understand that fear is . . . you know, scary! (It's there for a biological reason. Fear tells us when we should think twice, take a step back, worry.) So, how do we deal with this? How do we summon the confidence to dive into that swimming pool or start playing those notes?

Glad you asked!

Because the next group of animals are saying:

LET US PUMP YOU UP!

From the octopus to the beaver, we can learn so, so much from these creatures – partly because we're remarkably similar. OK, OK, there are *some* differences between you and a deer. (The fur! The antlers!) You're not *exactly* like a lion or a flying frog. Yet, just like the animals in this chapter, we all want to believe:

I can do this!

I can do this well.

And we all shouldn't be so hard on ourselves.

YOU DON'T HAVE TO BE PERFECT, YOUNG HUMAN.

YOU REALLY DON'T.

None of the animals in this book get it "right" all of the time. That doesn't make them any less miraculous – or any less self-assured. So, let them show you how sensitivity can be strength, how everyone has claws, and how you can build confidence – **leap after little leap.**

Focus on the things you're good at and **STOP COMPARING** yourself to others

As humans, we're perpetually peering from side to side, wondering if other people are performing "better" than us. No matter how good we might feel about ourselves, there always seems to be *someone* who's smarter, bolder, more popular – and we judge ourselves against them.

That's a real confidence killer!

What would happen if *animals* did this, if they constantly compared themselves to others?

SOMETHING TO CROW ABOUT

Meet 007, a wild crow captured for a short time by researchers in Australia. Here's a short list of things he can't do.

- HE CAN'T SWIM LIKE THE PENGUIN.

- HE CAN'T RUN AS FAST AS THE OSTRICH.

- HE CAN'T HOVER LIKE THE HUMMINGBIRD.

- HE CAN'T SLEEP WHILE FLYING, LIKE THE ALBATROSS.

- HE CAN'T DEVOUR WHOLE MICE LIKE THE OWL — OR ROTATE HIS HEAD 270 DEGREES.

- HE CAN'T SPEAK HUNDREDS OF HUMAN WORDS LIKE THE AFRICAN GRAY PARROT. (IN FACT, 007 CAN'T SAY ANY HUMAN WORDS.)

And those are just a few birds! Don't even get me started on lions, polar bears, great white sharks. Can you imagine a crow like 007 chasing down a wildebeest? Or trying to intimidate a seal?

See how silly this sounds?

007 *could* focus on all that nonsense. Or he could say to himself, ***these are all the things I can do.***

- I CAN SOLVE EXTREMELY DIFFICULT PUZZLES, LIKE GATHERING SMALL STONES AND STICKS AND USING THEM TO FISH OUT A SNACK.

- I CAN REMEMBER A HUMAN'S FACE FOR AT LEAST FIVE YEARS — AND EVEN PASS THAT KNOWLEDGE ON TO MY BIRDY FRIENDS. (HEY, LARRY! WATCH OUT FOR THE FARMER WITH THE BEARD! CA-CAW!)

- AND I CAN SEARCH INSIDE MY MIND — REFLECTING, PONDERING.

They're big thinkers, these birds. When a crow passes away, other crows surround the body – heads bobbing, eyes searching. Mourners in black, they've gathered to play detective. *How'd our friend die? How can we avoid being next?* And they're even helpful to other animals, if the viral story "Crow Helps Hedgehog to Cross the Street" is anything to go by. When a frightened hedgehog kept stopping in the middle of the road, a crow continuously pecked the hedgehog's back, nudging the creature to safety. *Peck! Come on, you're almost there! Peck! We'll make it together!*

See what I mean? See what might happen if a crow like 007 only compared himself to others? He'd miss all of those wonderful strengths.

As would the rest of these animals!

THE GUINEA PIG is NOT GOOD at fetching sticks like a dog. He's TERRIBLE at barking at the mail delivery person, and REALLY BAD at chasing the cat. And the guinea pig could feel quite awful about this (he's a household pet, after all, just like Fido, who *can* do all these things!), but then he remembers: I'm GREAT at learning! At three hours old, I was already starting to run. No dog could do that so quickly!

THE TASMANIAN DEVIL

is an AWFUL kicker, compared to her marsupial cousin, the kangaroo. She REALLY STINKS at batting away predators with her hind paws. But she is an EXCELLENT biter! What other marsupial can open her mouth eighty degrees? She can crush bone!

THE SLOTH is the WORST when it comes to

speed. Just look around the Yasuní National Park in Ecuador, where he lives! Look at all of those fast little ocelots, with their speedy kitty paws! He could NEVER run that fast. He can't even purr! But he's the BEST at pull-ups. How else could he hang from that tree all day? That sloth is over three times stronger than a human — and *certainly* stronger than an ocelot.

Everyone has their thing! Scientists call the crow a confident bird for what he *is*, not for what he isn't. Animals like guinea pigs, Tasmanian devils and sloths gain confidence by focusing on their strengths – not by dwelling on comparisons. When you start to travel down this road, telling yourself *I'm not as "good" as them*, just ca-caw to yourself. Think about 007 – who is probably very OK with his feathers, and with his problem-solving abilities, even if he doesn't growl as convincingly as a bear (or at all). Think about those guinea pigs, who will never fetch you a newspaper, or those sloths, who will definitely not be sprinting through the forest.

They're great as they are.

Recognize your CLAWS

Of course, to focus on your strengths, you first need to realize: *Oh, hey, those are my strengths!*

Now, you don't have to sport one-and-a-half-inch claws like the lion. You don't have to tackle an antelope or a wildebeest, or roar with a ferocity that shakes the grass. But everyone – absolutely *everyone* – has something like claws: tools that we use to display the excellence within us. Maybe you're a fantastic dancer. Maybe you have an exceptional sense of style. Or maybe you're great at listening and understanding how others feel.

Those are your claws.

Confidence is all about recognizing that you have them.

Take a moment to think about it:

WHAT ARE *YOUR* TOOLS? WHAT MAKES YOU FEEL POWERFUL? WHAT MAKES YOU ROAR?

WHILE YOU'RE THINKING, LET'S MEET CHRISTIAN.

In 1969, two humans found a young lion for sale in a London department store and decided to buy him and take him home. Christian grew rapidly (as lions tend to do!) and soon, he was just too big for their cramped London apartment. Those humans knew: *It's time to send Christian into the wild.*

But they were worried about this decision. Would Christian find his confidence? Everything would be frighteningly new to him! He'd never lived in Kenya before. He'd never asked a pride of lions: *Mind if I tag along?* Would he crumble under the pressure?

The humans released him, uncertain.

A year later, they returned to Kenya . . . and found that Christian had discovered his claws! By the looks of it, he'd recognized: *I'm actually really great at communicating with other lions. And I'm pretty good at leadership, too.* Before Christian enveloped his humans in a giant lion hug (aww!), they witnessed that confidence firsthand: He bounded over the savanna, surviving so beautifully in his new environment. He'd discovered the tools to display the excellence in himself.

Here's my point. Like Christian, you can have all the speed and intelligence in the world – but to have confidence, you also have to recognize those strengths, all of the wonderful qualities already purring within you. You have to acknowledge: *You know what? I am great at hockey. My cakes do taste delicious. I'm a really, really good friend!*

SO, WHAT ARE YOUR SHARPEST CLAWS?

EVERYONE HAS SOMETHING!

LEAP for it!

OK, your metaphorical claws are out! Now it's time for a leap.

For humans, leaps are all sorts of things: auditioning for the school musical, learning to snowboard, or even saying, "Hello, new person, I'd like to be your friend." They're moments when that skittering squirrel arrives, shouting, **POSSIBLE FAILURE AHEAD! REALLY, I MEAN IT, THIS COULD GO TERRIBLY! YOU SHOULD THINK ABOUT THIS FROM EVERY POSSIBLE ANGLE FIRST, OR BETTER YET, AVOID IT ENTIRELY!**

Sound familiar?

How often have thoughts like this stopped you from being confident? From trying new things?

THIS TINY FROG MIGHT HELP.

With their large toe pads and bendy bones, their webbed feet and extra skin, Wallace's flying frogs are built to glide, effortlessly jumping and parachuting from tree branch to tree branch. However, in order to successfully skydive, tree frogs still have to . . . you know, make the leap.

To give you some context, a Wallace's flying frog is – at most – about four inches long.

And it's jumping up to *fifty feet*, way up in the jungle canopy.

You can probably imagine what would happen if it misjudged the leap. (Injury, or worse.) And yet, before the big jump, these frogs probably don't think: *Do I trust myself to glide that far? Will I perfectly stick the landing?* No. Otherwise Wallace's flying frogs would stay on the same branch their entire lives. (Scientist would have to rename them! Wallace's stationary frogs? Wallace's non-swooping frogs?)

Young humans, these amphibians might say, **you can make the leap, if you trust your abilities – if you believe that your metaphorical feet are sticky enough.**

Because they are.

Besides, even if you fail, it's not like you're *literally* going to fall out of a tree. (A "no" from the school musical won't be nearly as bad as that.) You might wobble like a young mountain goat, before finding your footing on the rocks. You might stumble like a dolphin trying to tail-walk, before standing up firmly in the sea. But no matter what, you'll learn something, feel proud of yourself for attempting the jump – and you'll spring right back up again, ready to parachute through another day.

Confidence isn't always about
RUSHING IN

It's important to note that you don't have to make a leap *immediately*. You can think first and then act, like the octopus.

There's something so otherworldly about a giant Pacific octopus: reddish-pink, eight-limbed, and intelligent. They're massive, weighing up to 150 pounds – with more than two thousand suckers. And they're really successful, too, at all sorts of things! Taking lids off jars, using tools, hunting fish through mazes, squirting large clouds of ink . . .

A CREATURE LIKE THIS HAS EVERY REASON TO BE CONFIDENT!

Still, sometimes, it wavers, camouflaging itself into the background, coordinating its skin tone with the coral and rock. It sinks into the shadows, observing, away from it all. With nine brains and three hearts, the octopus can be a classic introvert. It thinks, thinks, thinks, feels. And that's amazing.

Google the giant Pacific octopus, and you might stumble upon a few videos of them interacting with scuba divers. In one, an octopus hangs back: *Hello? Who are you?* You can see him carefully assessing the situation. *Is this scuba diver dangerous? What is his purpose here?* And then, curiosity! One tentacle begins exploring the scuba suit. Soon, the octopus is all over the diver – in a nice way!

Do you sometimes hang back like this, observe before diving in?

That works!

Because when an octopus feels confident, he feels *extremely* confident.

Like this:

In 2016, at New Zealand's National Aquarium, an octopus named Inky boldly climbed out of his tank, saying *SEE YA* to the enclosure. *OPEN OCEAN, HERE I COME!* Suction-cupping his way across the floor, he slipped through one of the aquarium's pipes, escaping to the sea.

And this:

An octopus at the University of Otago *really* hated the lab's blinking lights. So, he kept squirting them with jets of water. Over and over again. *HA! HA! LOVELY DARKNESS!* This happened so many times that the researchers decided, "Too many power outages! Too pricey! Back to the ocean for you."

Definitely don't spray your light bulbs with water.

But *do* give yourself time to settle into things, into confidence.

THERE'S NO RUSH.

Listen to your "NO"

So, it's perfectly all right to sit back and observe before swooping in. However, what if you *don't* swoop in? What if you observe, observe – and then run away? It may surprise you to know that confidence is also about deciding *not* to do something. It's about listening to your "no" and trusting that choice.

Just like the deer.

"What?" I hear you saying. "What are deer doing in this chapter? They're super unconfident! They leap at the slightest twitch of grass, the softest snap of a twig! When cars curve around the bend, there they are: frozen in the middle of the road, a deer in the headlights."

Yeah, they're quite skittish.

They also – quite incredibly – trust their instincts. *Bad scent!* they might think. *Bad noise! Those are the footsteps of a hunter. Flee!* Some may say this is the opposite of confidence. The deer's running away! But look closer. That deer is leaping *thirty feet* over a stream – in one long stride. That deer is racing across the forest at almost *thirty miles per hour*, in the direction of safety. It's surviving in a very, very impressive way – because it had the confidence to listen to its own voice, which said, *This doesn't feel right.*

It's OK to be like the deer. In many ways, it's good to be like the deer. When something just feels off, it's OK to believe the animal inside you. This message might arrive in the form of

a whisper (*pssst, you don't need to watch that scary movie*), or a deep-down feeling in your gut (*SCARY! MOVIE! NO!*). Listen to it. Just as you can decide to leap, you can also decide: *Nope! No leaping in that direction, thank you!* That may not appear like confidence on the outside (not to others, at least), but it's actually one of the most confident things you can do.

Sometimes a deer sprints away at the sound of friendly footsteps. Sometimes a deer gets it "wrong." (*Oh, oops, that was just a farmer coming to feed me oats!*) And you might get it wrong occasionally, too. So what? When you make a choice based on the animal inside you, be gentle with yourself. You did the best that you could when you were trying to survive.

Build confidence one
STICK AT A TIME

That's it, then? You recognize your claws, listen to your inner animal, and *bam!* Supreme confidence? Well, that's half of it – but confidence is also a building game. It isn't about achieving immediate results; it's about persevering with tasks over time. Take a game like chess. Can you expect to be a confident chess player *instantly*? That kind of self-assurance might require years, and dozens upon dozens of games.

Now, beavers aren't great chess players (they'd probably gnaw the pieces), but they *are* perseverance experts. They've managed to survive, even when the odds were against them. In 1948, for example, the Idaho Department of Fish and Game decided to move a group of beavers to new ground. One government official developed a somewhat outrageous plan. Put 76 beavers in boxes. Strap those boxes to parachutes. And then drop them out of planes, directly over a wildlife sanctuary. Amazingly, the beavers were successful skydivers!

AND THEN THEY GOT TO WORK.

BEAVERS ARE ALWAYS WORKING.

In Canada's Wood Buffalo National Park, they've even built the world's largest beaver dam. No one had any idea it was there! Someone looking at Google Earth just found it one day! Twice the length of the Hoover Dam, the beavers' dam – manufactured from years' worth of woven sticks, waterlogged grasses, and fresh moss – turned out to be a whopping 2,788 feet long.

That took *years* of entwining sticks together. Under, over, under, over. Ten thousand pats of mud here. Twenty thousand smidges of moss there.

And that's really inspiring! These beavers have perfected the power of building things over time. They understand that nothing is accomplished all at once – that the world's largest dam is the journey of a million sticks. Sure, they might make a mistake here and there. A section of the dam might crumble (*Goodbye! It's been nice gnawing you!*). But those setbacks are part of a much bigger picture.

LITTLE ACTS OF CONFIDENCE TALLY UP.
YOU CAN ACTIVELY BUILD CONFIDENCE,
EVEN WITH THE SMALLEST STEPS.

You just need to give yourself permission to try – to take that first piano lesson, to play that first chess game, to chew that first stick. And then to keep your confidence going, even if you don't succeed at once.

YOU CAN DO THIS.

CONFIDENCE
IS ON THE INSIDE, BUT THE MORE YOU DEVELOP IT, THE MORE IT FLOWS TO THE OUTSIDE — THE MORE PEOPLE CAN GLIMPSE IT.

And, like laughter, confidence catches! When others see how self-assuredly you present yourself, they'll think, *Huh! Maybe I can do that, too.* That little seed of confidence can spread — from you, to your family, to your entire pack.

CHAPTER 3

DISCOVER YOUR PACK

BE YOURSELF – AND FIND THE
RIGHT FRIENDS FOR YOU

It's a rainy day in late spring, and two dogs are approaching each other in the park. One curves at an angle, tiptoeing through the mud, and one wags her tail happily to the right. At the same time, they bow, front legs outstretched – a chortle escaping them.

IT'S GAME ON!

They start to chase each other, wet coats shimmering, both understanding that *now, we're friends.*

Dogs can make it look so simple: strangers one minute, best buds the next. But really, there's a complicated system of communication at play. Those tail wags, those bows, are all part of an intricate friendship dance. What I'm saying is, animals get it.

THEY RECOGNIZE THAT GOOD FRIENDS ARE IMPORTANT, THAT THE WORLD FEELS BRIGHTER — AND LESS LONELY — WHEN YOU HAVE SOMEONE TO CHASE IN THE PARK.

Like us, animals form bonds for comfort, for joy, for a sense of community. Whether they're introverts or extroverts, whether they prefer alone time or travel in groups, animals offer a window into how we might approach friendship. How we might find a pack – or even a single friend – who appreciates our uniqueness and brings out the best in us.

Making friends, sometimes, feels like an unsolvable puzzle. What if someone doesn't like you? What if you're "no good" at meeting new people? What if there's "no room" left in the group? What if those "friends" turn out to be not so friendly?

HAVE NO FEAR!

Each and every animal in this chapter has been carefully selected to answer those questions – and to offer tips and tricks that might ease your mind.

So, without further ado, let's **dip** into the water with some **flamingos**, stroll by the river with a **capybara**, and **howl** along with a **pack of wolves**.

Be OPENHEARTED

Imagine an incredibly large guinea pig, with bristly brown fur, webbed feet, and kind eyes – *that's* the capybara, the biggest rodent in the world. Native to southern Brazil and other parts of South America, this exceptional animal made headlines when a group of them gate-crashed the Olympics in Rio, gently storming the golf course. Happily munching on greenery, they chilled out with the golfers and sunbathed in the sand traps, offering nothing but good vibes. Afterward, a host of newspaper articles settled on a common label: The capybara, they said, was

"THE FRIENDLIEST CREATURE ON EARTH."

Now, that's quite a statement! Capybaras have horses to compete with – and dolphins and dogs. But it's hard to argue with the capybara's approachability. From squirrel monkeys and crocodiles to chickens and other birds, like the yellow-headed caracara, all kinds of animals seem to feel at home next to the capybara. These barrel-shaped rodents even act as "nature's armchair," allowing smaller animals (and even other capybaras!) to hitch a ride on their backs.

SO, WHAT IS IT ABOUT CAPYBARAS THAT MAKES THEM SO FRIENDLY? WHY DO NUMEROUS SPECIES, FROM DIFFERENT WALKS OF LIFE, FLOCK TO THEM?

Capybaras are
openhearted.

When a squirrel monkey approaches on a riverbank, the capybara offers no judgment, no shame. She doesn't say, *We aren't meant to be friends, because you are who you are, and I am who I am.* Instead, she watches. She waits. She offers her back for comfort.

And that's a really vulnerable thing to do, right? Because what if the squirrel monkey runs away? What if you offer your friendship to a crocodile, and they turn around and bite you?

The capybara knows that being openhearted is risky. And yet, friendship is all about trust; it's about accepting people for who they are – and understanding that sometimes they'll disappoint you. Sometimes people *will* snap like a sharp-toothed crocodile. That doesn't mean that you did anything wrong. It just means you're trying.

If the capybara could speak in anything other than chirps, whistles, and barks, she might urge you to keep trying – if you're up to it.

KEEP THAT OPEN HEART, AND EVENTUALLY YOU'LL DISCOVER FRIENDS WHO'LL HAPPILY CLIMB ON YOUR BACK, AND WHO'LL EVEN OFFER YOU THEIRS.

ALONE TIME'S
OK, too

If the capybara is an extrovert, then koalas like Bill are definitely introverts. Bill isn't so social with the other marsupials in Wild Life Sydney Zoo. He spends a huge chunk of his life in solitude.

And that's his choice! You might not think it from Bill's cuddly appearance, but koalas are remarkably asocial by nature. Humans usually give names to groups of animals, like packs of wolves or flocks of flamingos. But there isn't a collective name for a group of koalas! It just doesn't happen often enough.

In fact, during the non-breeding season, these eucalyptus-eating introverts spend up to ninety-six percent of their time by themselves. That's an average of only fifteen minutes a day interacting with other koalas. While they *can* make noise – from soft clicks to burp-like roars – they often choose the tranquility of silence.

Similarly, there's the Eastern mole, who usually carves out tunnels only big enough for one. Somewhere in someone's backyard, a mole is digging up to sixty feet a day, living alone in a series of underground roads. Sometimes the only sign of him is a mound of fresh dirt, pushed up to the surface. He *can* meet with another mole, if he wants – but mostly, nah! He's good! Moles are so comfortable with themselves that they can exhale air – and then recycle it, breathing it in and out again and again.

Dear young humans, the koala and the mole might say, we understand if you want to stay home on a Friday night.

Nowadays, there's so much pressure to make friends, to have this picture-perfect social life to share online. But if you only want to hang out with people *occasionally* – or if you prefer quiet time like the koala – please don't feel awkward about that. In the animal kingdom, it's absolutely acceptable.

You might also think you're "no good" at meeting people.

Let's change that narrative.

MAYBE YOU'RE JUST *VERY* GOOD AT MAKING FRIENDS WITH YOURSELF. MAYBE YOU'RE BUILDING UP YOUR INTERESTS AND YOUR PASSIONS BEFORE SHARING THEM WITH THE WORLD. SO, WHEN YOU DO CLIMB DOWN FROM YOUR TREE — OR PEEK OUT FROM YOUR TUNNEL — YOU'LL KNOW YOURSELF BETTER.

And you'll understand what kind of friends you're looking for: humans who'll appreciate what you appreciate about yourself.

Pick people who
MAKE YOU HAPPY

Just for a second, let's go back to those two dogs playing in the park. Both of them were interested in a good old-fashioned game of *chase me, chase me!* They made each other laugh (a quick, panting *huh-huh* is basically doggie laughter). They were also pleased with each other's company – and probably felt happy about themselves. *I can run so fast! Look, my friend's brought out the best in me!*

WHAT I'M SAYING IS, YOU MIGHT WANT TO CHOOSE YOUR FRIENDS LIKE DOGS DO.

OR HOW BELUGA WHALES DO.

OR HOW ELEPHANTS DO.

YOU MIGHT WANT TO ASK YOURSELF THREE QUESTIONS.

DOES THIS PERSON SHARE MY INTERESTS?

If you were a beluga whale, you'd probably say, *HELLO, FELLOW WHALE! DO YOU ALSO LIKE BLOWING BUBBLES? I ABSOLUTELY LOVE BLOWING BUBBLES! FANTASTIC! LET'S DO THAT TOGETHER.* Or if you were a raven, you might question, *ARE YOU A FAN OF FROLICKING IN THE SNOW? SENSATIONAL! WHAT A FEELING! SO GLAD WE'RE ON THE SAME PAGE.*

DOES THIS PERSON MAKE ME LAUGH?

Just like common interests, laughter is a key component to friendship. It is for many animals, too. Some people might think that laughter is just a human trait, but over the years, science has proved: *THAT'S WRONG!* Dogs obviously get the giggles. Rats crack up when they're tickled. And when dolphins play-fight, they emit bursts of pulsed sounds (a quick series of clicks) and then a whistle. Essentially, this tells the other dolphin, *YOU'RE MAKING ME LAUGH! WE'RE NOT ACTUALLY FIGHTING! QUITE THE OPPOSITE: WE'RE BONDING.*

DOES THIS PERSON MAKE ME FEEL HAPPY ABOUT MYSELF?

This is perhaps the most important question. To answer it, you might want to consider elephants, who comfort their companions, who greet their friends with: *I'M GOING TO WRAP MY TRUNK AROUND YOURS.* And their friends cheerfully wrap their trunks right back. It's about togetherness — but it's also about happiness. It's about saying, *WHEN I SEE YOU, I FEEL GOOD INSIDE.*

If you've answered "yes" to all three questions, **congratulations!** You may've just found yourself a great friend.

Find a
NEW PACK

So, you've met a few humans who share your interests, and they're wonderful! They're warm, funny, kind – and you think, *I understand this whole friendship thing*. But what happens when you hit a roadblock? What happens if you try to make friends with someone and they don't like you back? What if you try to join a group and there's "no room" left?

AWOOO! AWOOO! AWOOOOOO!

(THAT'S WOLF FOR "LET ME EXPLAIN SOMETHING, HUMAN.")

Packs are a big deal for wolves. After all, it's rather hard to tackle an elk alone! Wolves need other wolves to support them – to help keep them safe and fed. Even little wolf cubs require companionship, someone to play with. How else can they learn those valuable hunting skills?

But group dynamics are tricky sometimes. Occasionally, individual wolves are so desperate for acceptance that they'll roll over on their backs, exposing their bellies to show they're not a threat. They'll crouch, tucking their tails, letting out a soft whimper.

Yet, wolves understand one crucial fact: **THERE IS ALWAYS ANOTHER PACK**. Always. If there isn't one readily available, you make one. Four to nine pack members is usually the sweet spot – but sometimes packs expand to thirty or more. From there, a few wolves decide: *You know what? I'm venturing off on my own. Who's with me? Cool. I'll find new company later.*

The same goes for baboons! A group of baboons, called a troop, is constantly changing. In and out, in and out – male baboons tend to jump from troop to troop, switching up their friends many times. And helmet jellyfish let themselves flow with the current, meeting up with new groups in their area. *Oh, hello, stranger! The water has brought us together. We're super-great swim buddies now!*

HERE'S THE TRUTH. ANIMALS DON'T ALWAYS GET ALONG WITH OTHER ANIMALS.

Not everyone will appreciate the talented, wonderful, unique human that you are. If a group closes its paws to you, if there's no room left in that part of the forest, it might sting for a little bit. You might tuck your tail for a day or two. But then you'll remember the wolf inside you, who's OK with venturing out on your own, with finding a *new* pack – one that brings out the best in you.

Good friends
HAVE YOUR BACK

After you've discovered that new pack, how can you be the best possible friend? Whether you're a zebra or a meerkat or an elephant, the answer's the same: Good friends stick together. They support one another in a million little (**and not so little!**) ways.

Let's look at a few animals that have one another's backs.

ZEBRAS!

Zebras are so supportive! In the wild, they clump together in herds — hundreds of them, all galloping across the grasslands of East Africa. And they very rarely fight. For five years, researchers in Africa studied a specific herd of plains zebras and witnessed zero instances of aggression among them. *ZERO*. Can you imagine not bickering with anyone in your family, with anyone from school, for *FIVE YEARS*?

They also act in defense of one another, as friends do.

Say that a lion attacks. Say he breaks into the herd, catching a zebra with his claws. The zebra's injured, afraid, crying out for help with a vocal call. Other members of the herd will answer: encircling the lion, clipping the ground with their hooves, chomping the air with their teeth. *BACK AWAY FROM OUR FRIEND! OR WE'LL KICK YOU! DON'T TEST US!* (Really, don't test them. Never stand at the kicking-end of a zebra. Their hind legs are tremendously powerful!) Eventually, the lion might step away from the injured zebra, slinking back across the savanna.

MEERKATS do something very similar — gathering around a predator (like a jackal) and hissing, *HEY, QUIT IT! STOP PICKING ON OUR FRIEND!* They'll claw at the jackal. They'll bite. And they have one another's backs in other ways, too. For example, meerkats live in large groups called "mobs" (no relation to the underground crime syndicates!) and often babysit one another's little ones. Individually, they'll also act as lookouts for the mob and call out to one another if there's danger: *HELLO, HELLO, BELINDA! WATCH OUT!* (OK, there probably isn't a meerkat named Belinda, but meerkats can say, "Oh, that's my friend's voice. I recognize it! I'd better flee!")

Of course, being **supportive** is more than just showing up during the bad times — during the lion attacks and the jackal confrontations. It's about showing up during **times of joy**, too.

We've already talked about the friendliness of dogs and the laughter of dolphins, so let's put the two together! In 2016, a Labrador named Ben met a dolphin named Dougie. It sounds like the beginning of some wonderful fairy tale, but it really happened. Many days, Ben the lab would dive into the sea — just off the west coast of Ireland, where he lived — and Dougie would be waiting. *Oh, the good dog is here!* Together, they'd play for hours, both swimming around, Dougie blowing bubbles and Ben trying to catch them. *Almost! Got it!*

Imagine Ben's legs paddling extra hard, keeping up with his dolphin pal. Imagine Dougie the dolphin clicking underwater, watching the dog's legs swishing above. It's quite the hilarious scene! And fun for everyone involved.

Occasionally, Ben would swim for a little too long, and Dougie would nudge his tired friend back to shore: *There you go, that's it, careful now.* They were entirely supportive of each other, encouraging each other's happiness. It was as if both dolphin and dog were saying, **YOU CAN TRUST ME. YOU CAN TRUST WE'LL HAVE A GREAT TIME TOGETHER.**

So, what are some ways that you can have your friends' backs? Listening is always a great place to start. That's where most animals start, anyway: training their ears toward the sounds of their group members and really hearing what they're saying. Maybe your friend's parents are going through a divorce, and she just needs someone to chat with – to surround her with support, like a zebra. Or maybe she just thought of the *funniest* joke, and she'd like an audience. You can be there to share that joy. You can be there through the good and the bad.

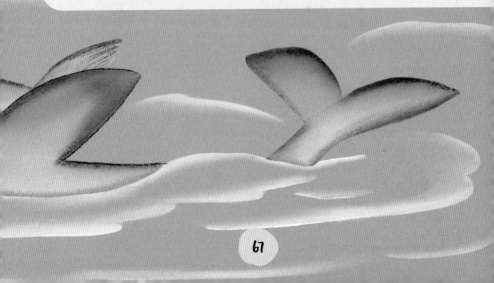

Expand your **FLOCK**

And finally, let's bring in the Chilean flamingos. They strut into the shallow water, thin legs bending, heads bobbing – and then raise their wings in salute, greeting one another. Unlike many other birds that have a hard time coexisting with other species, flamingos are super-accepting birds. A Chilean flamingo might see an Andean flamingo and say: *Hey, buddy! The good food's over here!* (Or, possibly, something like that in flamingo language. At the very least, a wing salute might be involved.)

Right now, scientists are actively studying flamingos – one of the world's most social creatures – to learn about lasting relationships. Ten million years ago, the flamingo's ancient ancestor stalked the Earth, so these technicolor birds have had a *long* time to figure out friendship. In fact, they're rather gifted at it. For up to fifty years – the average lifespan of a flamingo in the wild – they can maintain a core group of three or more friends. Sure, they "hang out" with their mates (their breeding partners), but they also spend quality time with other flamingos who enjoy their company.

REACH OUT TO YOUR FRIENDS, THE CHILEAN FLAMINGO MIGHT SAY. HONK TO TELL THEM, I'M WITH YOU.

They're constantly communicating! Like geese, Chilean flamingos are wonderfully chatty: howling and honking during flights, calling out to each other with their voices, so the flock can stick together.

But here, quite possibly, is the flamingo's greatest lesson: **Think about expanding your circle. A flock might be three birds. A flock might be thousands of birds.**

Scientists have observed that with bigger flocks, these birds were even more social with one another. More wing salutes! More calls! You've probably heard the expression "there are more fish in the sea." Well, there are more flamingos in the waterway. **IF YOU HAVEN'T FOUND YOUR FLOCK YET, TRY TO KEEP LOOKING. GIVE YOURSELF CHANCES TO BE FRIENDS WITH ALL KINDS OF PEOPLE.** That's what flamingos do. As their flocks grow larger and larger, so do their opportunities for friendship.

If you're comfortable, branch out a little. Join that extra club. Take that part in the school play. Spread your flamingo wings, and with time, you'll find a flock – or even one friendly bird – **that appreciates the best in you.**

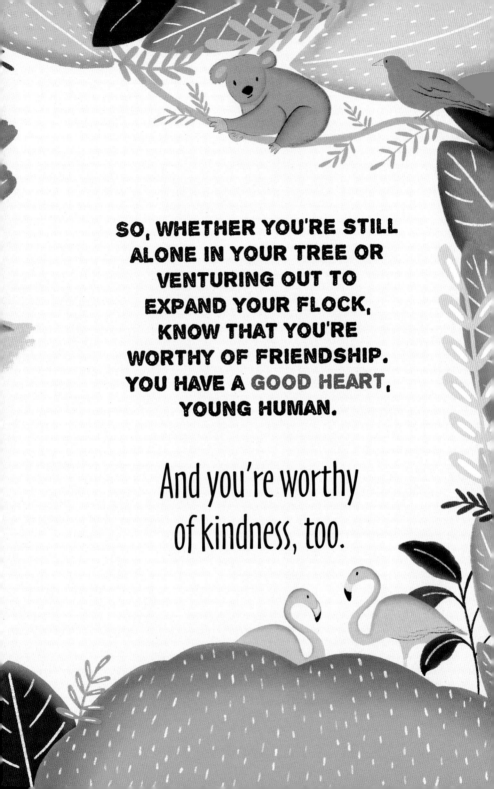

SO, WHETHER YOU'RE STILL ALONE IN YOUR TREE OR VENTURING OUT TO EXPAND YOUR FLOCK, KNOW THAT YOU'RE WORTHY OF FRIENDSHIP. YOU HAVE A GOOD HEART, YOUNG HUMAN.

And you're worthy of kindness, too.

CHAPTER 4

DIG A LARGE BURROW

BE YOUR KINDEST SELF

Author Henry James once said,
"Three things in human life are important:

the first is to be kind;

the second is to be kind;

and the third is to be kind."

Simply put, kindness is good for us! When we care about others, we're happier, healthier, and more connected. And yet, every once in a while, we might find ourselves in situations where kindness slips through our fingers – where we try, but don't measure up, to the gentle animal inside ourselves.

Maybe someone's bullying your friend, and instead of defending them, you jump in on the criticism. Maybe someone tells you a big secret, and instead of keeping it, you blurt it out in the cafeteria. Maybe you start a rumor about another person in your class – and it spreads around the entire school.

WHY DO WE DO THESE THINGS?

Sometimes it may feel like the only answer is to protect ourselves by hurting others. After all, that's what animals do . . . right? Just look at all of those nature documentaries. The leopard isn't exactly kind to the gazelle!

But that's an incredibly simplistic view of the world.

Yes, there's the whole predator-prey thing (some animals eat others to survive), but they never hurt one another for sport. They take no pleasure in bullying. Quite the opposite: Animals offer kindness to one another in countless ways, from burrow invitations to daring water rescues. Far from being an obstacle to their survival, kindness is one of the keys to their existence.

THINK ABOUT IT AS "SURVIVAL OF THE FRIENDLIEST."

Bottlenose dolphins, rats, orangutans – each animal in this chapter proves that animals are often hardwired for compassion. Kindheartedness isn't just a human trait. In fact, we can learn quite a bit from animals' careful, considerate behaviors: how they protect one another, how they accommodate others in challenging situations, even when they're at risk themselves.

THE WOMBAT WOULD LIKE TO GO FIRST.

Make space for **OTHERS**

In extremely difficult circumstances, how can we still find it in ourselves to offer kindness? How can we look around and say, "I know I'm hurting, but I'd like to help others who are hurting, too"? On the darkest nights, think of the wombat – a nocturnal animal with a penchant for digging. Stubby-legged with a wide set of sharp claws, their bodies literally barrel through the tough Australian soil, scooping up to three feet of dirt in a single evening.

Now, the wombat is first in this chapter for a significant reason.

THESE MARSUPIALS OFFER KINDNESS WHEN OTHERS NEED IT MOST – EVEN WHEN THEY'RE IN DANGER THEMSELVES.

In 2019, you may have seen news about the devastation in Australia: Massive bushfires raged across the country, killing over **one billion animals**. That's a staggering, heart-wrenching number. Mr. Rogers once remarked, when bad things are happening,

"LOOK FOR THE HELPERS."

And during the bushfires, wombats were the helpers.

Small animals took refuge in wombat burrows – far below ground, where the intense heat couldn't reach them. They rode out the destruction in those roomy caves, under the watchful eye of their marsupial neighbor.

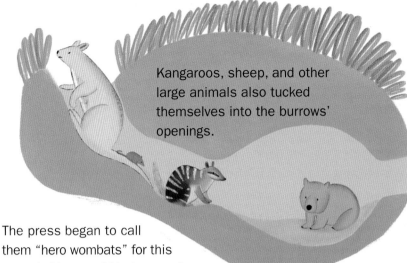

Kangaroos, sheep, and other large animals also tucked themselves into the burrows' openings.

The press began to call them "hero wombats" for this remarkable act of kindness – for hosting others at a time of unimaginable strife.

It's perhaps unsurprising, then, that the collective noun for wombats is "wisdom." **A wisdom of wombats.**

Here's an incredibly important detail that many news stories missed: These stocky marsupials aren't natural hosts. Far from it! They can be tremendously grumpy and fiercely defensive of their burrows. *Get out of my space*, the wombat often says to intruders, biting and swiping with its claws.

So, why did the wombat let down its guard during the bushfires?

KINDNESS. TOLERANCE. A RECOGNITION THAT THINGS ARE BAD AND WE'LL GET THROUGH THIS TOGETHER.

It would have been very easy for the wombat to boot out the intruders. Begone, birds! Sayonara, echidnas! It would have been easy for the wombat to think *the only one I should save is myself*. But the wombat made room. The wombat let them stay.

In trying times, this creature might teach us, *consider letting outsiders into your burrow.*

OFFER empathy

As a member of the animal kingdom, you're kind by nature. It's true! Researchers have proved that animals from white mice to chickens are determined to offer empathy, which is one of the best ways to show kindness.

Here are three experiments with rats, for instance – all of which actually happened.

A RAT learns that pressing a lever gives her tasty food. *YUMMY, A SUGAR PELLET!* Then, researchers switch up the game. When that same rat presses the treat–lever, it shocks a rat in a neighboring cage. *OUCH, THAT LOOKS LIKE IT HURTS.* She stops pressing the lever. The possibility of food isn't worth harming another creature. Even two pellets of food aren't worth it!

OH, NO! A rat's cage-friend is stuck in a thin, plastic tube: squirming and squeaking, whiskers twitching. A few days ago, the "free" rat was trapped inside that same narrow space. She remembers what it felt like: incredibly claustrophobic and stressful. And so, she thinks, *I ABSOLUTELY MUST GET YOU OUT OF THERE.* Her nose sniffs around the tube. *WHAT IF I TEST THIS LATCH? WORK THIS SPRING? GOT IT!*

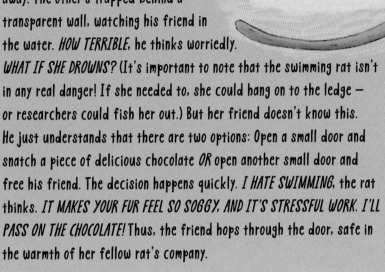

INSIDE A clear container are two rats. One's treading water, tail swishing, her little feet paddling away. The other's trapped behind a transparent wall, watching his friend in the water. *HOW TERRIBLE,* he thinks worriedly. *WHAT IF SHE DROWNS?* (It's important to note that the swimming rat isn't in any real danger! If she needed to, she could hang on to the ledge — or researchers could fish her out.) But her friend doesn't know this. He just understands that there are two options: Open a small door and snatch a piece of delicious chocolate *OR* open another small door and free his friend. The decision happens quickly. *I HATE SWIMMING,* the rat thinks. *IT MAKES YOUR FUR FEEL SO SOGGY, AND IT'S STRESSFUL WORK. I'LL PASS ON THE CHOCOLATE!* Thus, the friend hops through the door, safe in the warmth of her fellow rat's company.

What do all of these experiments have in common? (Besides the fact that humans aren't always so nice to animals!)

That's right: **empathy**.

In each, the rat's saying:

OH GOODNESS, I'VE BEEN WHERE YOU ARE, AND I KNOW HOW IT FEELS. HERE, LET ME ACTIVELY TRY TO

HELP YOU.

What are some other ways that animals offer empathy?

ORANGUTANS

Have you ever heard the phrase "laughter is contagious"? That's true for humans — but it's also the case with orangutans! These brightly colored great apes are highly social, and they often like to tickle each other. (Being tickled is pretty funny to an orangutan!) Their mouths drop open, which is their equivalent of laughter. *HA, HA, HA!* When another orangutan sees this gaping mouth, her mouth will stretch into that shape, too. This mimicry happens within a split second. See? Laughter catches. And, according to scientists, that's empathy. We laugh when our friends laugh, because we're connected with them — because we care.

PRAIRIE VOLES

If you've never seen a prairie vole in the wild, they look a bit like a mouse (with some hamster mixed in), and they're *EXTREMELY* empathetic toward their cage mates. In one experiment, researchers separated two vole partners and put one in a rather distressing situation, which his partner couldn't see. When reunited, that partner consoled the distressed vole. *OH, NO! WHAT HAPPENED? HERE, LET ME TRY TO MAKE IT BETTER.* In vole language, consolation involves grooming: licking backs, rubbing faces, washing ears. It's heartwarming to see how much they want to help.

ELEPHANTS

At heart, elephants are helpers, too, offering empathy to members outside of their own families, their own groups, and their own species. In zoos, keepers have witnessed Asian elephants consoling African elephants, saying *THERE, THERE* with a sweep of their trunks, and the last twenty years have delivered many, many accounts of wild elephants who came across a suffering peer — and didn't turn away. Far from it. Elephants lean in. They pull one another's calves from ditches. They refuse to leave struggling strangers who might be lagging behind the herd. *I WILL STAY WITH YOU*, they seem to say. *I KNOW HOW YOU'RE FEELING, AND I'M HERE.*

We can't always identify with others' experiences. But sometimes, we can reach inside ourselves and remember a moment when we've felt stressed, or sad – or even tremendously joyous. We can share that with others, saying: *I understand, I've been there, you are not alone.*

That takes courage. It takes wisdom. And it also takes practice.

But you're kind by nature.
You've got this.

Practice random
ACTS OF KINDNESS

If we're talking about kindness, *we must* talk about dolphins. Did you know that dolphins are one of the smartest animals on the planet? The way they communicate is unbelievably impressive. **They click! They whistle!** Dolphins might even have unique dialects in different parts of the world. Because of their astonishing intelligence, humans have studied their brains quite thoroughly. And we've learned that dolphins are really sensitive creatures. They can think, *I get it. I understand what you're going through, even if you're not a dolphin like me.* Perhaps that's why dolphins practice

 random acts of kindness.

In 2007, surfer Todd Endris was riding his board in the waters of Monterey Bay, California. What else lives in Monterey Bay? Bet you thought I was going to say dolphins!

Those come later.

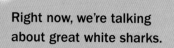 **Right now, we're talking about great white sharks.**

One of these sharp-toothed predators charged out of the water, biting Todd quite badly. He would've probably died if not for . . . Yes, you guessed it now. **A pod of bottlenose dolphins!** Witnessing Todd's grave danger, the dolphins sprang into action: chasing off the attacker, encircling the surfer and helping him return to shore.

Perhaps even more amazingly, Moko – a much-loved dolphin at a beach in east New Zealand – heroically saved two miniature sperm whales. Stuck in shallow water, the mother and her calf risked death if they didn't return to the deep sea. In her animated, dolphin way, Moko guided the pair farther, farther, out to safety. *Follow me! Thank you! You're welcome!*

These aren't isolated incidents. Throughout history, dolphins have maintained a habit of randomly showing up to offer a helping flipper. Just look at the ancient Greeks, who wrote about dolphins' protective qualities – or tale after tale of swimmers who, right before they nearly drowned, were rescued by a friendly face. A *very* friendly face, actually. With their curved mouths and tiny, pearly teeth, dolphins always look like they're smiling.

What's so wonderful is, dolphins didn't have to do any of this. They probably didn't *plan* to offer kindness to other animals – animals *outside* their own species – but when they saw an opportunity for compassion, they dived in.

HERE ARE A FEW
OTHER ANIMALS WHO
DIVE IN, TOO.

CROW GIFTS

What's your most valuable possession? Is it a baseball glove passed down from your grandfather? Or the science trophy sitting on your bedside table? Perhaps it's that little piece of sea glass gifted by a crow? The last one might seem a bit odd! But crows have a history of delivering tiny gifts to their human friends, especially when food is involved. Back in 2015, newspapers across the country swooped in on the story of Gabi Mann, a young American who was quite popular with crows. Before school, she'd scatter peanuts and dog kibble in her backyard. *WHAT TASTY NIBBLES*, the crows seemed to say, thanking her randomly in return. Every once in a while, Gabi would find a gift left by the crows, specifically for her: a bead, a button, a rotten crab shell. (Rotten crab shells, a crow might assume, are quite the prize!) Now she has an entire collection — piece after piece of kindness.

DONKEY NIBBLES

As humans, we might not think, "I know what I'll do for my friend! I'll comb their hair. That'll make them super happy." But in the rest of the animal world, grooming is often a kind act. Picture it with me: There are two donkeys in a field. One saunters up to the other, in that boisterous donkey way (*HULLO! HULLO!*), and starts spontaneously nibbling her friend's neck. Donkeys adore a good scratch.

I'LL PROTECT YOU, BIRD!

Just when you think it's impossible to love dogs even more, you learn about their bird-rescuing ways. Turns out, all across the world, they have a history of adopting feathered friends. For instance, here's a Labrador named Doug, with nine baby ducklings on his back. He's like their foster dad — a role that he randomly assigned himself, after the ducklings were abandoned.

So, what are some ways that you can dive in? Perhaps you could write a letter to an elderly neighbor. Or make breakfast for a family member. Or give your dog extra belly rubs (if he likes belly rubs!).

NOW MORE THAN EVER, THE WORLD NEEDS KINDNESS — AND YOU CAN HELP SPREAD IT,

ONE RANDOM ACT AT A TIME.

Reach across
DIFFERENCES

So, you're performing random acts of kindness like a crow, and you're offering empathy like an orangutan. Great work! But there's more. Being your kindest self also means being inclusive: reaching across differences and extending kindness to people who might not look, act, or think like you. We've seen this with dolphins and whales, with a Labrador and those little ducklings, but a baby hippopotamus and an aging tortoise are here to underline the point!

WHAT DO A HIPPO AND A TORTOISE HAVE IN COMMON?

Not a great deal! Both *do* enjoy a good splash in the water, but these species aren't natural friends. Yet, friendship is exactly what happened in Kenya, after a disastrous tsunami swept a poor baby hippo out to sea. Saved by quick-acting locals, the baby (named Owen, after his primary rescuer) found comfort in the presence of a tortoise. As soon as the little hippo scurried into the Kenyan wildlife park, he darted *straight* for Mzee, a 130-year-old giant tortoise, and swiftly cowered behind him. You can probably imagine what that tortoise was thinking, seeing a 660-pound hippo calf charge at him like that! (*Oh no, I'm dinner!* Or an annoyed, *Who let this guy in*?) In fact, Mzee seemed rather peeved by Owen's presence. *Why are you following me everywhere? Don't you have something better to do?*

Baby hippos display this cowering behavior with their mothers – loping behind them, hiding beneath them. Soon, Mzee realized: *This little guy doesn't mean any harm. He's pretty nice, actually.* And so, the tortoise began extending kindness to the hippo: sleeping by his side, playing with him. Miraculously, the pair even created a language of head nods and different sounds to communicate with each other.

Owen needed Mzee. And Mzee reached across their differences to extend a helping hand. (Or, you know, a helping set of toes and claws!)

If a tortoise and a hippopotamus can practice inclusivity, then you absolutely can, too. (All of the people you meet are just that: people! You don't even have to bridge the species gap.)

And you never know when you're going to meet your NEXT GOOD FRIEND.

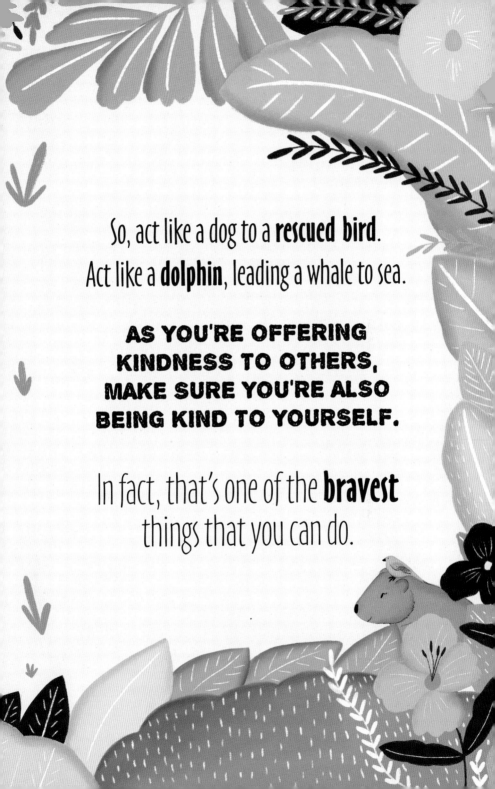

So, act like a dog to a **rescued bird**.
Act like a **dolphin**, leading a whale to sea.

**AS YOU'RE OFFERING
KINDNESS TO OTHERS,
MAKE SURE YOU'RE ALSO
BEING KIND TO YOURSELF.**

In fact, that's one of the **bravest**
things that you can do.

CHAPTER 5

SHOW YOUR SPIKES

DISCOVER YOUR BRAVERY

Discover your **BRAVERY**

As humans, we often think of courage as a rare resource. Bravery, we might believe, belongs to an elite few: rescuers who run into burning buildings, astronauts who rocket into space. But really, courage can be quieter than that – and it's certainly more abundant than that. In fact, it's everywhere. **We *all* have courage within us** – the ability to face something even if it's frightening – and to understand that we need look no further than the animal kingdom.

Sometimes, we overlook the bravery of animals because, well, they can't really write books about their daring deeds! (On the library shelves, there are no titles like *The Bold Adventures of Mr. Cheetah* by Mr. Cheetah.) We also don't always recognize their courageousness for what it is. We don't see a hedgehog exposing its belly and think: *Wow, what bravery! The gallantry of that hedgehog!* And yet, a tremendous amount of courage was wrapped up in that decision to belly roll. From the tiniest mammals to the biggest reptiles, animals are infinitely courageous – nearly every day of their lives.

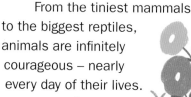

AFTER ALL, IT'S NO COINCIDENCE THAT THE TERM "LIONHEARTED" IS ANOTHER WAY TO SAY *COURAGEOUS!*

YOU ARE LIONHEARTED, TOO!

We often perform acts of courage without realizing that we're being brave. (We go to the dentist, for example, even if we're a bit afraid. We take those school exams, even if we're dreading them.) This chapter's about harnessing that power within you – and coaxing it out a little further.

Let's start with the polar bear and work our way through ten other animals that display astonishing courage. Some, like harpy eagles, you might expect. Others, like butterflies and dairy cows, might surprise you. Hopefully they'll prove that bravery often comes from unexpected places, and that you have the ability to conquer anything that darts your way. By the end of this chapter, you'll learn the importance of acknowledging your fears, leaning on your friends for support, and building your strength with individual acts of courage.

So, are you ready to be *your* bravest self?

TAKE A DEEP BREATH, LIONHEART – AND TURN THE PAGE.

Decide what's worth
FIGHTING FOR

Though anything we do that involves
overcoming fear can be called brave,
sometimes we need to choose our battles to achieve
what's most important to us, as well as the world around us.

Polar Bears Fight for Their Young

I think we can all agree that polar bears are rather brave.
Don't they thrive in the Arctic, one of the world's most extreme
environments? Even the way they *move* feels unstoppable,
like they could quite literally tackle anything. We can learn so
much from these snow-white predators, not least that they
make good use of their courage, summoning it at times of
high importance – such as when the survival of their loved
ones is at stake.

A polar bear will fight passionately for her
cubs – even against members of her own
species. In 2017, *National Geographic*
wildlife photographers captured
images of a fierce mama bear
and her twin cubs. Deep in the
Canadian Arctic, the trio stomped

across the shoreline – waiting for the ice to refreeze, so they could hunt. While waiting, a hungry male bear approached, threatening them. Weighing in at over 1,100 pounds, he could have easily overpowered the cubs *and* their mother. But still, the mama bear charged, diving toward him, nose first. *"Back! Back!"* Charging, grunting, teeth flashing, she threw herself between her twins and the intruder. And it worked!
The angry male skittered away.

The mama bear wasn't fearless.

Her bond with her cubs was just *stronger* than fear.

Geese are the same way – relentlessly protecting their young. Never cross a mother wolf, either! She'll throw any hesitation out the window, if she thinks her pups are in even an ounce of danger. Claws out! Teeth out! *Grrrrrr!*

COURAGE EXTENDS FAR BEYOND THE PARENT-OFFSPRING RELATIONSHIP, THOUGH. THERE ARE SO MANY WAYS THAT ANIMALS SHOW THEIR COURAGE WHEN SOMETHING IMPORTANT TO THEM IS THREATENED.

Koalas Fight for Their Homes

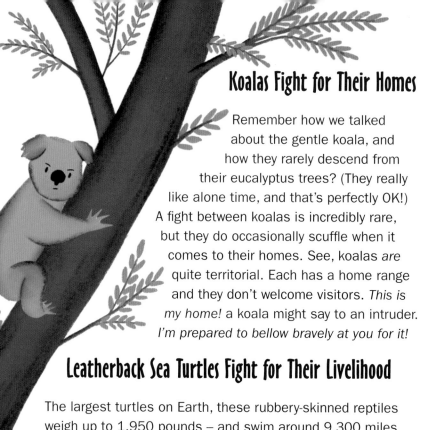

Remember how we talked about the gentle koala, and how they rarely descend from their eucalyptus trees? (They really like alone time, and that's perfectly OK!) A fight between koalas is incredibly rare, but they do occasionally scuffle when it comes to their homes. See, koalas *are* quite territorial. Each has a home range and they don't welcome visitors. *This is my home!* a koala might say to an intruder. *I'm prepared to bellow bravely at you for it!*

Leatherback Sea Turtles Fight for Their Livelihood

The largest turtles on Earth, these rubbery-skinned reptiles weigh up to 1,950 pounds – and swim around 9,300 miles per year. That's an astoundingly long journey! So, why do they undertake it? Why swim with the killer whales (who might say: *Mmm, turtle snack!)* and risk getting caught up in fishing nets?

Leatherbacks understand that the destination is worth any fear. *In the spring, my livelihood's at risk on the coast of Indonesia. There just aren't enough jellyfish! Better pack my suitcase . . .*

OK, we know that turtles don't have suitcases!

BUT THE IDEA REMAINS: On the Pacific coast, there will be plenty of jellyfish to fill their turtle bellies. No matter what danger they face during migration, turtles find courage within themselves; keeping their population alive is the most important thing.

What do *you* think is worth fighting for? What's worth your bravery? Could it be standing up for a cause you believe in – like climate change, which is impacting the polar bear? Or maybe it's telling someone: *Hey, I like you.* (Being vulnerable and placing your feelings on the table takes courage, too.) So, tap into your inner polar bear, your inner leatherback turtle, and decide what's worth fighting for. Imagine that you're tough like them, unstoppable like them – because guess what?

YOU ALREADY ARE.

We're all afraid of
DIFFERENT
THINGS

As you're tapping into your inner brave animal, you may want to consider what you're afraid of, and which situations really require your courage.

Most of us are afraid of getting hurt. That's entirely rational! You might hesitate before swimming in the sea, because there are stinging jellyfish in there (and unlike the leatherback turtle, you don't find them appetizing!). Or, you might hesitate on your bike at the crest of a hill, because what happens if you tumble?

But some of our fears are unique to us – and some aren't so logical. Perhaps you're afraid of spiders or . . . I don't know . . . pillows! Or feathers! Or feather pillows! It's not always big things that are scary.

The dairy cow knows this only too well.

What's that? Oh my goodness, what's that? A SHADOW! Oh, no. A CLOCK! Oh, no. SUDDEN MOVEMENT! Is that A NEW FEED STATION? It's too shiny, too echoey, too different! Dairy cows really don't like the sight of an unfamiliar object or a dark shadow creeping across the floor. All of these things will send a cow scuttling to the back of the barn!

To us, a dairy cow's fears might seem a teeny bit silly. *It's just a shadow! It's just a clock! It's just a feeding station!* We might think: *Let's change the name "scaredy cat" to "scaredy cow."* But that's unfair, isn't it? Things that seem harmless to us are *sincerely* frightening to a cow. And, if we look closer, the cow starts to do something really brave.

By backing away, she is acknowledging her fear.

She's saying: *Yes, I'm afraid of this.*

But look. Now she's starting to move toward the shadow, the clock, or the feeding station. She's facing her fear. She's brave!

Similarly, some horses get frightened by their saddles! Some dogs are terrified by balloons. But after they've recognized those fears, they can start to see: *Hey, this isn't so bad!* That saddle, or balloon, won't hurt them, after all.

Even if you're afraid of something small or seemingly insignificant, the fear is real to you. And acknowledging it is the first step to overcoming it.

BUT IT CAN TAKE TIME TO CONQUER OUR FEARS COMPLETELY.

You could start SMALL

OK, so – you're trying to tap into your inner polar bear, and you're beginning to understand the importance of telling fear: *I see you.* That's wonderful! But please don't feel like you need to be instantly brave all at once. Start small, with one modest act of courage that lays the foundation for bigger, bolder acts.

For example, Bretagne the golden retriever didn't start out as a hero. She began her life as a floppy, curious puppy – bursting with enthusiasm. But two years later, she'd act as a search-and-rescue dog on one of history's biggest recovery missions, on the day known ever after as "9/11" – the day two planes, hijacked by terrorists, flew straight into New York's World Trade Center and its twin towers collapsed to the ground. Brave Bretagne sniffed through the rubble for up to twelve hours at a time, trying to find survivors, as chaos swirled around her.

So, how did she jump from puppy to hero?

With careful training, Bretagne was taught to focus on special tasks – sniffing for specific smells. She was encouraged to shut out loud, scary noises around her and concentrate on identifying what was most important to the task. Bit by bit, Bretagne learned that by channeling her instincts and not letting external dangers distract her, she could cope with the scariest of situations.

A golden retriever and a harpy eagle are quite different! (I think that most dogs would be a bit frightened if they had to nest like an eagle – so high up in the Peruvian treetops.) But in at least one way, they're similar: Harpy eagles practice courage with small steps, too.

One of the world's most powerful birds, these super-predators have talons like a bear's and can take down a sloth without much effort. Looking at them – at the way they swoop and dive so bravely – you'd think this bird was born courageous.

But it started inside their nest.
Peeping over the edge – for five or six months.
Until, finally, the chick took a small, shaky leap.

So, let's say you're afraid of standing up and speaking in front of your class. What would be a good first step to overcoming your nerves? It could be first practicing in front of a friend or a family member. Then, just like brave Bretagne, bit by bit you can learn to focus on your main task and not what might be going on around you.

You can conquer that fear with just one paw step,
one little leap.

Vulnerability is
STRENGTH, TOO

So, if you're practicing courage, then where does vulnerability come in?

First, let's define what vulnerability actually means, because I think a lot of humans get it wrong. If you're vulnerable, you're presenting your true self to someone. You're saying: *I'm letting you in, even though I'm a bit scared to.* It's an incredibly brave thing to do! So often, humans think that vulnerability is a weakness – that we can't cry in public, for example, or share what's in our hearts – because we need to keep our guard up in case we get hurt, right?

WRONG!

We know that being able to protect ourselves from real threats is important. This is something the little hedgehog knows very well. Despite their easily swallowable size, these spiny mammals can fight off deadly vipers.

Quills – made of a stiff protein called keratin, like a human's fingernails – coat a hedgehog's back. When threatened, hedgehogs curl themselves into tight little balls, protecting their soft, pink bellies. *Ha, you can't hurt me when I'm like this. Just try it!* Getting past those quills would be very painful for predators like foxes. That's over 5,000 sharp spikes, all poking into you!

BUT HEDGEHOGS ALSO UNDERSTAND
THE POWER OF OPENING UP

and of letting people see their soft underbellies.
Just as they can courageously defend themselves,
hedgehogs can also choose to lay down their quills; they
can let themselves be vulnerable – which is equally brave.

Pet hedgehogs often like to have their tummies stroked.
(A nice belly massage feels quite relaxing after a long day of
being a hedgehog!) But, to make that choice, these pets have
to decide: *Do I trust this human enough to rub my belly?*
Will they hurt me? Or can I let myself be seen? Soon, they'll
relax their muscles, laying their quills flat.

That's **courageous** of them!

They're presenting their whole selves – and letting people in.

By allowing yourself to be vulnerable from time to time, you
can experience that happiness, the kind that comes from your
true feelings being met with understanding and love. Like a
hedgehog, you have those quills when you need them, but it
often feels better – and braver – to keep them down.

Lean on your **HERD**

Being brave doesn't mean going it alone. Sometimes, even when we have huge hurdles to leap, we think: *I've got this. I can do this by myself. I'm strong!* But other times, we need help. And what's more, we are designed to work as part of a team, to help one another out! Why make a solo leap when others might be willing to stand by your side? (Or *walk* by your side, if you're a caribou. We'll get to that in a second.) The point is, you can and should lean on your herd: your friends, your family, your community. Say, for example, that you'd like to champion a cause at your school, such as free lunches or animal rights. Wouldn't you feel just a *little* bit braver with a supportive friend defending that cause right next to you?

Animals show us, time and time again, how courage blooms in numbers.

Just look at caribous, the world's most migratory land mammal. Let's follow their journey from summer to winter – from the tundra, filled with bristly grass and hardy fauna, to a more protected climate, with snow falling gently on lichens. What do you notice about them besides those spectacular antlers? (Did you see the size of those things?) You might observe how closely they stick together – and how far they travel in a herd. Porcupine caribou pad their hooves across 3,100 miles of land in a single year. That's over 200,000 *individual* caribou zigzagging through fields and over rivers. It can be a treacherous journey.

And it's growing more treacherous with time.

Every year, a greater number of pipelines pop up. So do roads. So do other man-made obstacles. And individual caribou scare quite easily. They pause by the obstacles and seem to think: *Nah, nope, no way! Not crossing that!* Only with the courage of a group, it appears, do they successfully navigate these obstacles. You can almost hear them egging one another on, saying: ***I'm right here! I've got your back! You're not doing this scary thing alone.*** Together, they stream across the barriers, proceeding peacefully on their journey.

Caribou are far from the only creatures who find strength in numbers. Many animals that we've already discussed – like capybaras and Chilean flamingos – rely on one another for that extra boost of courage. But it doesn't hurt to talk about a few more!

The Weight of Butterflies

Like the caribou and the leatherback turtle, monarch butterflies are migratory animals, but they're *quite* a bit smaller. On average, a single monarch weighs only a third of an ounce. Yet, together with thousands and thousands of members of its species, this insect undertakes one of the longest, most difficult journeys in the animal kingdom: from the United States and Canada to Mexico. Along the way, these butterflies roost, clustering together for safety – *leaning* on one another, and protecting their flutter from the cold.

Whoop, whoop!

 According to *The Lion King*, hyenas are pretty cowardly, but this just isn't true! A close cousin of the mongoose (and not even remotely related to dogs!), spotted hyenas carefully and courageously plan their hunts, calling together the whole pack with a distinctive: *"Whoop, whoop!"* You can hear that noise roll across the savanna. It might mean: *We need to intimidate this lion! ASAP!* Or it might mean: *Get here so we can tackle this zebra!* No matter what, it's a call to arms – a call for bravery as a group. *We're stronger together than apart!*

So, don't be afraid to lean on your herd.

Maybe you're doing a charity run or entering a challenging competition or even battling an illness. Let your friends, family, and community help you where they can. Let them strengthen you with their bravery. After all, I'm sure you'd do the same for them.

Together or apart, it takes an **ENORMOUS** amount of **COURAGE** to survive in the face of uncertainty and change.

And you're doing really well! Even reading this book – and thinking about these big topics – shows just how courageous you are.

KEEP PADDLING AWAY IN THE WATERS OF YOUR LIFE.

Keep going, young human, even when the waves are rough.

CHAPTER 6

KEEP SWIMMING

FIND THE RESILIENCE THAT WILL KEEP YOU GOING

Life can be terribly unpredictable. Life can change in the flap of a wing, in the flick of a whisker. Sometimes that means wonderful change that we aren't expecting. Sometimes we're faced with awful things, completely beyond our control – and all that's left for us is to adapt, to pick ourselves up again, to keep swimming. Now, I'd like to tell you something good. Something excellent, actually!

Just as you are a **brave**, kind, unique individual by nature, you're also **naturally resilient**.

(YOU'RE STILL HERE, AREN'T YOU? YOU'RE READING THE PAGES OF THIS BOOK!)

But occasionally, we also need a little encouragement in order to keep going. That's where the animals of this chapter excel. From the red foxes of London to a horse named Zippy Chippy, they'll provide a few models for coping, for perseverance.

They'll show you that rainy days will probably pass, that you can ask for help, and that you should let yourself feel all the things – including grief.

These animals will even hold your hand. (Metaphorically speaking, of course. I'm not sure you'd actually want a vampire bat to snuggle up to you. And you may think twice before holding paws with a skunk!)

As you're going through this chapter, remember that everyone copes differently – because everyone *is* different. You might be more like an orca or more like a raccoon. You might find inspiration in the Louisiana black bear, in a baby pangolin – or even in the tiniest fire ant. But hopefully you'll come away from these stories with a greater sense of resilience.

It's a tough world out there. The last few years have proved this more than anything.

BUT THE FOX IS READY!
ZIPPY CHIPPY IS READY!

THEY'LL HELP YOU WEATHER THE STORM.

Think about
ADAPTING TO CHANGE

One of the most difficult things we have to face as humans is change. We learned in the last chapter about the tremendous journeys of the caribou and the monarch butterflies, and how they find strength in numbers, but we haven't yet talked about animals who adapt to great changes, like landscape or climate. This is really important, because your life will inevitably be full of transformation: Maybe you'll change schools or towns or even countries. Maybe your family will grow or shrink. How will you respond to those shifts? Will you adapt? Or fight against them?

THE FOX KNOWS:
CHANGE HAPPENS ALL THE TIME.

Once, the habitat for red foxes in the United Kingdom was exclusively in the countryside. There, they happily stalked chickens and other small prey, content in the willowy grasses –

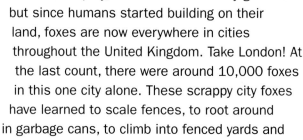

but since humans started building on their land, foxes are now everywhere in cities throughout the United Kingdom. Take London! At the last count, there were around 10,000 foxes in this one city alone. These scrappy city foxes have learned to scale fences, to root around in garbage cans, to climb into fenced yards and

snack on whatever's available. *Mmmm! Half an egg sandwich! Nice!*

One particularly adaptable fox (nicknamed Romeo) even lived on the seventy-second floor of the United Kingdom's tallest skyscraper, The Shard. Evidently, he crept up a stairwell during construction and was rather sneaky about pilfering food scraps from the workers. For a while, he had the best view of the city! Obviously, when Romeo was discovered, The Shard's staff carefully escorted him out, but he proved that foxes can survive almost anywhere, no matter how much change they encounter.

YOU SHOULD KNOW, YOUNG HUMAN, THAT YOU'RE VERY MUCH LIKE THE FOX.

You are a wise, adaptable survivor.

You are capable of endurance – of finding ways to thrive in new landscapes. So, when change comes along, consider how you might treat it as a growth opportunity. As a chance to show how strong you are. Of course, this isn't always possible – or preferable. But you might just find yourself, fox-like, basking in the sun of a different habitat.

Keep picking
YOURSELF UP

Once you've discovered how you can adapt like the fox, the next step is learning how to pick yourself up. To *keep* picking yourself up – over and over again. When was the last time you said something like: *I can't do it any more!* Or: *I might as well just quit!* In school, maybe you're finding a foreign language really tricky, or you can't quite seem to wrap your head around math. Maybe you've been working *extra* hard to make the basketball team, but your dribbling skills aren't where they need to be. It's so tempting to throw in the towel . . .

OR THROW IN THE SADDLE,
IF YOU'RE A HORSE.

I'D LIKE TO INTRODUCE YOU TO A HORSE NAMED ZIPPY CHIPPY, a Thoroughbred from upstate New York. Humans typically praise horses (like Zippy Chippy's great-great-uncle, Secretariat, or his cousin, Man o' War) for their racing prowess, their tremendous speed. They fly along the track! Leap around the bends!

But Zippy Chippy is famous for a rather unusual reason:

Everyone recognizes him as the
biggest loser in racing history.

He never won a *single* race. That's right, Zero! Goose egg! Once, live on TV, a human even beat him in a race. A human! On two feet! When the race was well underway, Zippy Chippy  was still at the starting line, glancing around, taking too long before realizing: *Oh, are we racing now? Right! Let me get on that.* And he was often more concerned with sneaking snacks and nipping at his coaches than with racing. By the end of Zippy Chippy's career, his record stood at a staggering 0–100.

THE THING IS, THOUGH, ZIPPY CHIPPY
LOVED TO RUN,
HIS MANE FLAPPING IN THE WIND.

He adored the track, and – according to his trainer – was always ready to go. No matter how many times he lost. No matter how many times he'd have to pick himself up. For Zippy Chippy, the only direction was forward. **(And, occasionally, to the side – when he didn't quite remember where he was going!)**

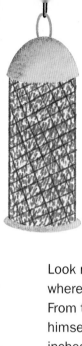

It's hard to top Zippy Chippy in the perseverance category, but squirrels certainly give it a go!

Every one of them keeps thriving in the face of failure.

Look no further than a backyard in North America, where a squirrel patiently waits to pounce on a bird feeder. From the top of a fence, he calculates his jump, then FLINGS himself toward the seeds – missing the mark by several inches. No worries. Like cats, squirrels always land on their feet and can fall safely from dramatically tall heights. And they're comically determined. The gymnasts of the rodent world, they'll learn to swing from that slippery pole. They'll ricochet off that fence – even if it takes a few attempts. No task is too daunting when walnuts are involved! (Squirrels are huge walnut fans.)

In 2020, one YouTuber – a former NASA engineer – even built a squirrel obstacle course in his garden. The objective? Outwit these rodents! Save the birdseed for the birds! The course, which included (among other hurdles) a maze, a wobbly bridge, and several long jumps, appeared nearly impossible. But guess what? These clever squirrels kept working at the obstacles.

Whenever they failed, they hoarded that knowledge, tucking information away like walnuts in their cheeks. Eventually, after a week of constant failure and constant effort, **SUCCESS!** *Ha ha ha!*

VICTORY NEVER TASTED BETTER.

Now let's travel to Berkeley, California – where, in 2016, researchers studied twenty-two wild fox squirrels. They trained them to open a tiny, rodent-sized box. Inside was a savory snack! *Well, this is easy*, the squirrels probably thought. *It's not even a bird feeder! I don't even have to hang by my toes!* But soon, the researchers stopped putting walnuts in those boxes. The squirrels went ballistic! *Where's my food? What kind of trick is this?* Frustrated, they tried to obtain the nut in other ways: turning over the box, knocking on the box, chattering.

That's really important.

Essentially, although they'd "failed" at their task, these quick-thinking animals attempted a different approach. *What if I tried this? Or this?* They innovated! They learned new skills. If a constantly losing horse can still race with such joy, if squirrels can brush away failure and innovate – then you might be able to pick yourself up, too.

Sometimes, it's not about winning at all. It's about how much heart you give it.

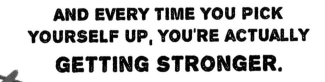

AND EVERY TIME YOU PICK YOURSELF UP, YOU'RE ACTUALLY GETTING STRONGER.

This'll probably **PASS**

What happens, though, when things are utterly overwhelming? What happens when you don't have the energy to keep picking yourself up? That's a really understandable feeling – and it's absolutely nothing to feel ashamed of. Sometimes we just *can't*.

But there's hope – even if your head's stuck in a storm drain.

Or if you're covered in mud at the bottom of a very deep hole.

RACCOON RESCUE

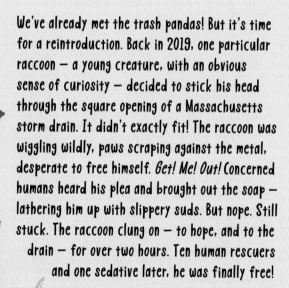

We've already met the trash pandas! But it's time for a reintroduction. Back in 2019, one particular raccoon — a young creature, with an obvious sense of curiosity — decided to stick his head through the square opening of a Massachusetts storm drain. It didn't exactly fit! The raccoon was wiggling wildly, paws scraping against the metal, desperate to free himself. *Get! Me! Out!* Concerned humans heard his plea and brought out the soap — lathering him up with slippery suds. But nope. Still stuck. The raccoon clung on — to hope, and to the drain — for over two hours. Ten human rescuers and one sedative later, he was finally free!

THE GREAT SKUNK ESCAPE

A year earlier, in California, two skunks were in a similarly tricky spot. In the middle of the night, they'd tumbled into a construction-site hole, falling several yards. At the bottom, mud gripped their bellies, their paws. As you can imagine, it was not a happy moment for these skunks! Come morning, a human noticed the animals with a gasp — and immediately gathered a rescue team. Extracted from the hole, one skunk rebounded quickly; the other (cold, shivering, with a fractured tail) took a little longer to recover. But he did! He survived, returning to his feisty self the very next day.

All animals have stuck-in-a-hole moments — when things appear hopeless, when their fur is terribly matted with mud. Not everything passes so quickly (or at all). Sometimes those experiences become part of us, and like foxes, we have to find ways to adapt.

BUT PLEASE REMEMBER THAT MANY BAD THINGS PASS.

When your head's stuck in a storm drain, you might be a few hours away from release. When it's winter and you're trembling in your burrow, spring is just around the corner.

Let yourself feel
ALL THE THINGS

Through bright days and not-so-bright days, allow yourself to feel – *really* feel. Maybe you're OK with embracing those happy emotions (*Yay! We're adopting a cat this weekend, and I am PUMPED!*), but how do you react when a storm arrives? Do you let yourself experience sadness, too, or is it easier to shut out everything (and clam up like . . . well, a clam)?

Here, the orca wants to chime in.

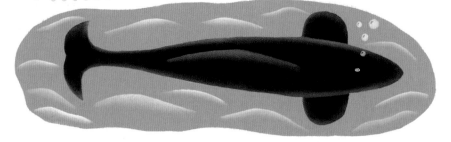

Which isn't terribly surprising, because orcas – also known as killer whales – are quite chatty! A whistle here. A pulsed call there. Occasionally, they'll add a bubble display, pushing air through their blowholes. They also, very notably, live their emotions out loud – refusing to shy away from their grief. Instead, they let the whole ocean witness it.

In 2018, an orca named Tahlequah helped scientists understand how deeply whales feel. For seventeen days – in the waters outside Seattle, Washington – Tahlequah held on to the body of her calf, who'd passed away. She never pretended that her grief didn't exist. She never said, *I'm fine* in her whale language.

She just let herself **feel everything.**

Orcas aren't the only animals who throw themselves into grief. Giraffes do, too – often splaying their legs to bow and nudge their dead. Elephants hold vigil over their fallen, ears drooping, gathering sticks to blanket the body. When Gus the polar bear lost his mate at the Central Park Zoo, he took to the water, swimming lap after sad lap – rejecting any toys that the zookeepers tried to send his way. And I think we can learn from them, from every single one of these animals. We might think we aren't "supposed" to express sadness – or anger, or betrayal.

BUT A BIG PART OF RESILIENCE IS BEING TRUE TO YOURSELF. AND THAT INCLUDES BEING TRUE TO YOUR FEELINGS.

Try not to hide them. Try not to bottle them up. It's healthier to be like orcas, like elephants, like giraffes. Otherwise, how can anyone know that you're suffering? How can anyone offer help? And how can you keep swimming, with all of those emotions trapped inside – weighing you down?

We need to feel those hard things, so we can grow stronger because of them.

You can ask for
HELP

Remember how we talked about leaning on your herd when you're trying to be brave? Resilience in the animal kingdom often means doing the same thing: seeking out friends, family, or members of your community, and asking them, *Will you help?*

It is very OK to ask for help! It doesn't signal that you're weak. Quite the contrary. It signals that you have enough strength left for wisdom – enough power to recognize when you can't entirely manage alone. You might be stuck in a metaphorical hole like a skunk. You might be grieving like an orca. Or you might be a little down on your luck, like an extra-hungry vampire bat.

I know! The words "help" and "vampire" don't traditionally go together. But hear me out! When vampire bats feed, they only take a teeny-tiny bit of blood from their prey; they don't *truly* harm anyone. And their female communities are especially close-knit. Did you know that if a vampire bat doesn't feed for two days, she's at risk of starvation? That's so quick! And it's not always possible to score that nightly meal.

Not to fear, though! Another female has it covered, literally swooping in.

Essentially, all a vampire bat has to do is show: *I'm pretty hungry; I need help.* And presto! One of her friends will vomit up her own dinner, sharing some. Yes, OK, it's kind of gross. But it's also incredibly generous. What's more, these sharing moments happen all of the time. According to researchers, vampire bats actually *build* their communities – at least in part – on this help-giving. They remember who fed them on those hungry nights, understanding: *I can rely on you, friend! And now you can rely on me, too. When you've missed a meal, come straight to my part of the cave.*

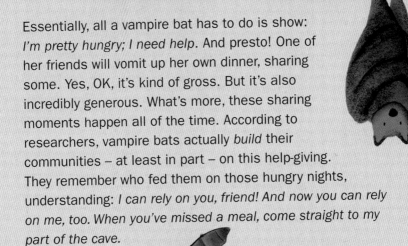

YOU'RE TOUGH — BUT YOU'LL BE EVEN MORE INVINCIBLE IF YOU REACH OUT.

If you ask for a helping hand or paw or wing.

DON'T WORRY: CHANCES ARE YOUR FRIENDS WON'T BITE!

It's possible to BOUNCE BACK

Have you ever heard of a phoenix? A red bird with extraordinary wings, it catches fire, burning to ashes. Then it grows again, rising from the cinders – alive and thriving once more. While the phoenix isn't a *real* bird (it only exists in Greek mythology, and in our imaginations), this magical creature is like a number of animals who face life-altering experiences and bounce back, as strong as ever.

A COLONY OF FIRE ANTS.

When hurricanes hit the United States, flooding communities and washing away plant life – leaving only a plain of water in their wake – these tiny insects stick together. Literally. Like otters "holding hands" while rafting, fire ants link their legs, joining together with *10,000* of their closest friends. Using their naturally waxy bodies and a work–sharing system (*You go on the bottom of the raft! Now I go on top! Now switch!*), ants float together, riding out the storm. And once the floodwaters recede, they carry on as usual.

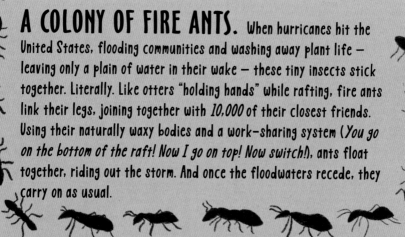

LOUISIANA BLACK BEARS.

In 1992, the US Fish and Wildlife service declared this creature "threatened." Many animals who enter endangered species lists never leave them. Luckily, these bears are excellent foragers (acorns and pecans and beetles, oh my!), and they can adapt to a wide variety of landscapes, even hostile ones.

Strong, stocky legs let them flee dangerous areas while massive claws allow them to hunt in their new homes. It's true that humans helped rebuild part of this creature's habitat, but really, the Louisiana black bear deserves credit for its own survival — and for doubling its population!

HOPE FOR HOPE! If you've never heard of a pangolin, think of an anteater with scales — and you're about to meet one right now. This is Hope. In 2020, a villager found him on a roadside in Thailand; The poor pangolin was alone, malnourished, and only a month old. But Hope was a fighter. Little by little, he mustered the strength to eat a few ant eggs. Then a few more. He found that resilience within himself — the thing that said, *keep eating, keep exploring your enclosure, keep your pangolin chin up.* Soon, Hope recovered.

It's possible, young human. It's possible to bounce back.

You're much more resilient **than you think.**

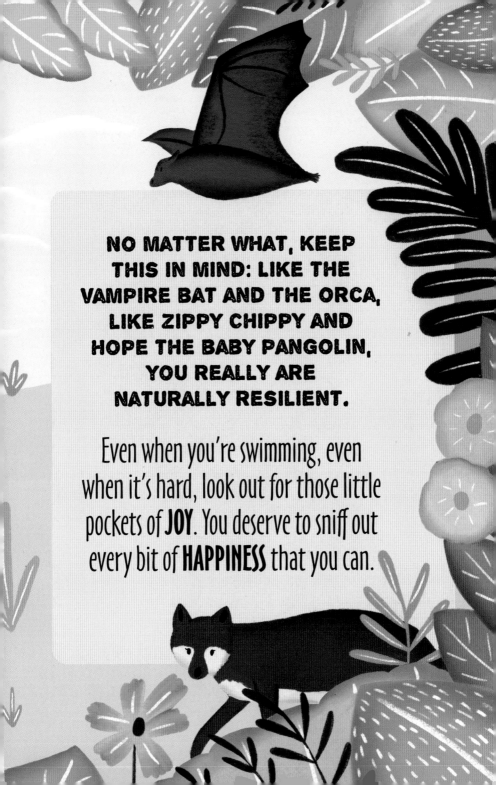

NO MATTER WHAT, KEEP THIS IN MIND: LIKE THE VAMPIRE BAT AND THE ORCA, LIKE ZIPPY CHIPPY AND HOPE THE BABY PANGOLIN, YOU REALLY ARE NATURALLY RESILIENT.

Even when you're swimming, even when it's hard, look out for those little pockets of **JOY**. You deserve to sniff out every bit of **HAPPINESS** that you can.

CHAPTER 7

SNIFF OUT JOY

BE HAPPY!

Somewhere in the middle of America, a dairy cow has a choice: She can travel out of her barn, through a dark path filled with shadows, or she can take the bright path, lit up with sunshine. Can you guess which one she chooses?

The sunny one!
Always the sunny one.

Like us humans, many animals are instinctively drawn to brightness. We often seek out things that make us feel good on the inside, that bring us warmth and joy.

Yet, on certain days – or maybe even a lot of days – we aren't especially happy. I want to say, up front, that some humans find it much easier to be happier than others.

Really, everyone's different! The world around us also impacts our levels of happiness, and it's quite understandable if you feel glum about things that you can't easily change.

But I've got excellent news for you! According to most researchers, **the best way to live joyously is just to be yourself**. You're a marvelously rare human, remember? Continue to embrace that! Keep reminding yourself that you're unique, **YOU'RE KIND, AND YOU'RE WORTHY OF EXCEPTIONAL FRIENDSHIP**. Find the people, places, and activities that bring you happiness – and hold on to them tightly, like Congo held that paintbrush, remember?

In this chapter, we'll talk about *even more* ways to sniff out joy. Beginning with dogs (who are remarkable sniffers!) and leading up to pot-bellied pigs and pandas, we'll dive into happiness like a golden retriever chasing a ball. (That is, very enthusiastically!) And we'll think about techniques that might make our world a little brighter:

like counting the little joys along with the big,
learning the importance of **self-care**,
and **RELISHING** every ear-flapping moment.

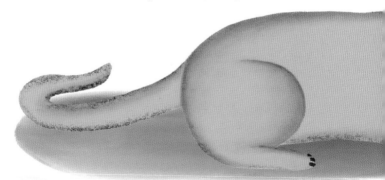

Sit and Stay in the
MOMENT

The world is full of wonder. Just ask dogs! At the sight of a biscuit, they wiggle their behinds and dance and shake. When their humans come home from school, dog tails whip around like windmills – faster, faster, *faster* – until their hindquarters are a perfect blur. What's a dog's secret to happiness? How can our metaphorical tails wag as fast as theirs?

Here's an answer.

ALL DOGS LIVE IN THE MOMENT.
ALL DOGS FOCUS ON THE HERE AND NOW.
THEY LET THEMSELVES JUST *BE*,
WITHOUT WORRYING SO MUCH ABOUT
THE PAST OR THE FUTURE.

Altogether, humans are particularly bad at this! How many times a week do you wonder: *Is everyone having fun without me?* When you're doing something enjoyable, like riding your bike on a garden path, how often do you stop and fret? *I have that huge math test on Monday*, you might think. Or: *Will anyone sit with me at lunch next week?*

Wouldn't it be great if we could live in the moment, like dogs? If we could breathe easier, laugh more freely, appreciate the world around us?

You can, human! a pup might say.
Try these things the *DOG WAY*.

EMBRACE THOSE EAR-FLAPPING MOMENTS.

Have you ever seen anything more joyous than a dog sticking her head out of a car window, jowls flapping, ears quivering in the breeze? What about a dog crunching on a peanut butter treat, or chasing a seagull across the beach? They're fetching joy! Make sure you're embracing those experiences in your own life. Stay in those moments and let yourself really feel them.

FOCUS ON THE BALL, BALL, BALL, BALL, BALL...

Sometimes it helps to laser-focus on one particularly joyous activity. Dogs do it all the time. Like with sniffing! The next time you're watching a dog in the park, notice the way his snout twitches in the air, catching every delicious scent. Notice the eager position of his tail, the way he's completely focused on the smell. He can easily spend fifteen minutes sniffing the same patch of earth. Rabbit urine? He's *on* it. Chipmunk poop? *Oh boy, that's the best.* Occasionally, he'll even get his paws involved, dredging up the scent, dirt flying in magnificent arcs.

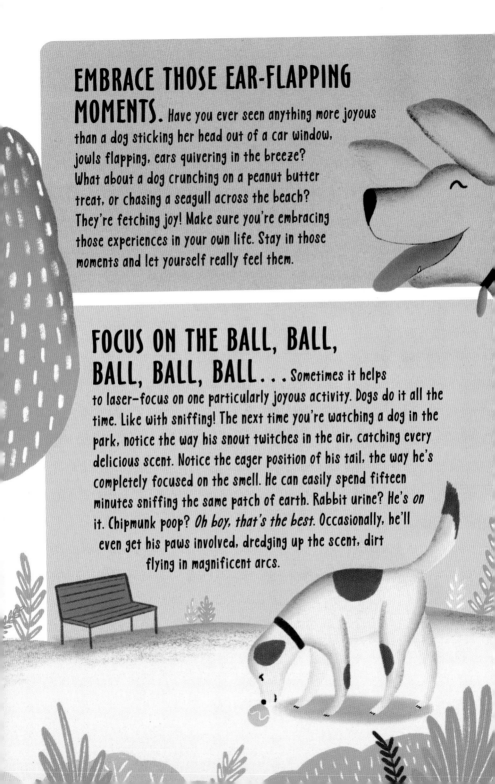

Don't even get me started on tennis balls! Mud-coated tennis balls. Brand-new tennis balls. The extra-chewy ones with blue stripes down the middle. A dog might lurch after every one of them, ears flopping with absolute glee. And when he catches them, he probably isn't thinking about his next grooming session. He isn't thinking about the past or the future. Most likely, he's only thinking about the ball, ball, ball, ball, ball.

SET YOUR PHONE ASIDE
(except if it's a squeaky toy).

These days, nothing kills the moment like a cell phone. Ask yourself: *Do I feel happier when I look at social media? Or does it take me away from the joyful things I'm presently doing?* Unless it's covered in peanut butter, or makes the sound of a doorbell, a cell phone is of little use to a dog. Pull a phone from your pocket, and your dog might think: *Darn! Why isn't it something better? A beefy treat. Or a nice chew toy, with a squeaker in the middle.*

So, think about spending a bit of time away from your phone and a bit more time in the present moment (say, playing fetch with a dog!).

BE STILL (OR, *STAY!*)

Part of being present is learning to be still. Dogs are quite gifted at this! Watch a dog on a warm summer's day, when the light is falling gently on the grass and the world feels deliciously slow. Maybe their eyes are closed. Maybe their ears are twitching softly against the wind. They're basking in that stillness, letting themselves just *be*.

Next time you have a spare moment, close your eyes and pretend you're a dog on a warm summer's day. You can pick any dog you'd like! A golden retriever. Or a Jack Russell terrier. Or a bulldog. All that matters is you're calm, and still, and allowing yourself to rest comfortably.

You may notice, sometimes, that other thoughts barge in.

Such as, *SQUIRREL!*

A squirrel charges across the path of your mind. Maybe several squirrels. Maybe an *army* of squirrels. But here's the thing: You don't always have to chase them. You don't have to rush after them into the bushes, snapping branches along the way. Think to yourself: *Why yes, that is a squirrel*, and let it skitter away.

Then use your sniffer to take big, deep breaths.

Little joys
COUNT, TOO

When you're living in the moment, like a dog, you'll also start to notice the joy of little things. Often, we're taught to believe that only the big joys count – for example, the birth of a new sibling, or winning a championship soccer match.

But small joys are
just as important.

After all, they're happening every day, all around us – and they can add up to a whole lot of happiness.

Here. Let the elephant and the pot-bellied pig show you.

For an elephant, a **BIG JOY** might be reuniting with a family member after a long period apart. *It is so, so, good to see you!* Rushing at each other with a series of trumpets, ears flapping and trunks high in the air, they'll greet their lost relative with fanfare. But elephant reunions don't happen every day! Instead, there are **LITTLE JOYS.** There's slipping into a nice spot of mud and coating themselves with the coolness. There's the delicious munch of a fig, the wonderful squish of a mango.

ELEPHANTS REALLY LOVE FRUITS AND VEGGIES!

And there are quick games with friends, tails swish-swish wagging like dogs.

If you're a pot-bellied pig, a **BIG JOY** might arrive in the form of a new pigpen. A wonderful pen! Clean and spacious, with a deep bed of straw, plenty of places to forage, and – of course – a few playmates. Every day, though, there might be **LITTLE JOYS**. Some pigs relish a good belly rub, dropping on their side and lifting their legs into the air. They love to play, too – and snuggle, and swim, and sleep nose-to-nose, feet flitting with dreams.

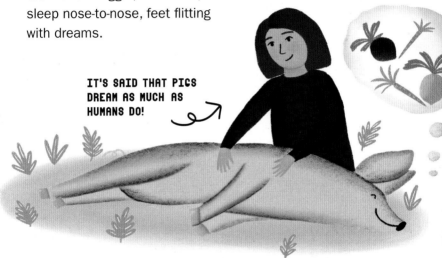

IT'S SAID THAT PIGS DREAM AS MUCH AS HUMANS DO!

So, relish the big things – those moments that bring you tail-wagging, trunk-trumpeting joy. But also remember the everyday moments, the ordinary things, that fill up your heart. They can be anything, really! Maybe you've made a warm mug of hot chocolate and you're thinking: *Wow, this tastes truly delicious!* Maybe you're curled up with a fluffy blanket, listening to the sound of rain, and you're just *so* comfy. Those things – all of the little things that brighten our days – count, too.

THE MORE WE NOTICE THEM, THE HAPPIER WE BECOME.

Take care of yourself
PLAYFULLY!

If you're going to keep swimming, that takes energy. If you're exploring your bravery, that takes effort. In fact, many of the topics discussed in this book require quite a bit of work! And it's seriously important to balance that with self-care. We all need the time and space to rest, to refill our wells. If you've had an especially challenging week at school, for example, you must let yourself recover. Sometimes, that comes in the form of a skip around the park in the sunshine. Or a long bubble bath, with extra bubbles. It comes from showing yourself love, attention and care.

As you might've guessed, self-care isn't just for humans!

➡ Animals, too, benefit from rest and relaxation.

Watch a kangaroo gently lounging in the dirt, or a hippo pressing her belly to the earth. Think about tigers, who spend almost sixteen hours a day asleep – rejuvenating their bodies and their minds with kitty *Zzzzzzs*. And grooming! Of course, grooming serves an evolutionary function (otters, for example, clean their fur for buoyancy, and crows keep their feathers nice and spiffy, in flying shape), but grooming can also be relaxing. Domestic cats often lick their stomachs to chill out. According to one study in the United Kingdom, Barbary macaques go a step further: All they have to do is witness one of their friends being groomed, and suddenly, they're wonderfully calm. *Matilda seems pretty chill from that back cleaning! So, now I'm chill, too.*

And then there's play.

A big part of taking care of yourself is carving out time for **GOOD, PLAIN FUN**. I promise, you'll be happier for it! When we play, we're tapping into our creativity, relieving stress, and soothing ourselves. So, take a playful page from these animals' books.

KOKO AND HER KITTENS
➡️

Koko the gorilla could sign all sorts of words, like "hot," "soft," and "cat." She *really* wanted a cat friend, and was firmly unsatisfied with a stuffed-animal version. One year, on her birthday, Koko's keepers surprised her with a litter of kittens — and she was overjoyed! Oh, how they played! Obviously, Koko was substantially larger than her new kitten friends, so she gently placed one on her head. And let another one softly scratch her back. In the end, Koko even got to keep two of the kitties. That way, they could play whenever they wanted — not just on her birthday.

SNOW DAYS AND SLIDES!

In February 2019, when the weather grew cold in Washington, DC, two giant pandas — named Mei Xiang and Bei Bei — took turns somersaulting down the powdery hills of the Smithsonian's National Zoo. *Yes! Yay! Wheee!* In between tumbles, these black–and–white bears — their fur misted with snow — plopped down to enjoy a hearty bamboo snack. Then they got right back up and somersaulted some more.

Pandas seem to love a good slide — whether it's down a hill or on a playground. Jia Yueyue and Jia Panpan, who call the Toronto Zoo home, also took turns pushing themselves down a bright yellow slide. *Do you think this is fun? I think this is tremendous fun!* One after the other, they tumbled to the bottom — and immediately started play–wrestling, kicking up the entertainment another notch.

and spiffy, in flying shape), but grooming can also be relaxing. Domestic cats often lick their stomachs to chill out. According to one study in the United Kingdom, Barbary macaques go a step further: All they have to do is witness one of their friends being groomed, and suddenly, they're wonderfully calm. *Matilda seems pretty chill from that back cleaning! So, now I'm chill, too.*

And then there's play.

A big part of taking care of yourself is carving out time for **GOOD, PLAIN FUN**. I promise, you'll be happier for it! When we play, we're tapping into our creativity, relieving stress, and soothing ourselves. So, take a playful page from these animals' books.

KOKO AND HER KITTENS

➡️

Koko the gorilla could sign all sorts of words, like "hot," "soft," and "cat." She *really* wanted a cat friend, and was firmly unsatisfied with a stuffed-animal version. One year, on her birthday, Koko's keepers surprised her with a litter of kittens — and she was overjoyed! Oh, how they played! Obviously, Koko was substantially larger than her new kitten friends, so she gently placed one on her head. And let another one softly scratch her back. In the end, Koko even got to keep two of the kitties. That way, they could play whenever they wanted — not just on her birthday.

SNOW DAYS AND SLIDES!

In February 2019, when the weather grew cold in Washington, DC, two giant pandas — named Mei Xiang and Bei Bei — took turns somersaulting down the powdery hills of the Smithsonian's National Zoo. *Yes! Yay! Wheee!* In between tumbles, these black-and-white bears — their fur misted with snow — plopped down to enjoy a hearty bamboo snack. Then they got right back up and somersaulted some more.

Pandas seem to love a good slide — whether it's down a hill or on a playground. Jia Yueyue and Jia Panpan, who call the Toronto Zoo home, also took turns pushing themselves down a bright yellow slide. *Do you think this is fun? I think this is tremendous fun!* One after the other, they tumbled to the bottom — and immediately started play-wrestling, kicking up the entertainment another notch.

MEERKAT SCUFFLES

For a long time, scientists thought that "play" was nature's way of saying: *Get ready! Fighting times are ahead!* Predators honed their claw-batting skills on their siblings. Turns out, though, play-fighting doesn't make animals any better at hunting! Look no further than meerkats, who punch and bat and scratch and scuffle — for fun! These rowdy antics never translate to increased hunting skills. Meerkats play because they *want to*. They play because it restores or opens something within them.

So, what kind of self-care can you practice today? Yes, today! What are the ways that you love to play? Can you borrow an exciting book from the library and spend the rest of the afternoon cuddled up on the couch, lost in a fictional world? Can you go for a swim outdoors, or sit quietly by yourself for a few minutes, just focusing on your breath? What about doing something kind for a friend, like baking them cookies? (Practicing kindness can absolutely be a form of self-care!) At a bare minimum, drink plenty of water (like a cow or a cat or an elephant), hit the hay when you're sleepy (as many barn animals do), and unclench your jaw when you're stressed. In the wild, creatures pay attention to what their bodies need – and what their fun-loving hearts need, too. A rule for life!

Spend time with
NATURE

Now, let's combine everything in this chapter! One of the best ways to sniff out joy – to find happiness in little things, to live in the moment, to take care of yourself – is to spend time with nature. There's a reason why an ancient Greek doctor named Hippocrates (not to be confused with "hippopotamus"!) said that "Nature itself is the best physician."

IT'S HEALING! IT'S CALMING.
IT REMINDS US THAT WE'RE
ALL PART OF SOMETHING
MAGICAL AND WONDROUS.

Of course, a miniature goat wants to butt in here!

Because there are some rosebushes in the distance – and she'd like to investigate. Crossing the field, hooves thudding over the dry earth, she plops a bundle of flowers in her mouth, back teeth chomp-chomping. *A little thorny, but not bad! Not bad at all! Now, where to next?* She explores the pasture, reveling in all the sights, sounds, and smells. Miniature goats are notorious escape artists, squeezing their small frames under fences and through the narrowest opening in a barnyard gate. Perhaps they like to experience as much nature as possible – other pastures, other forests, other tasty rosebushes.

And did I mention the sunshine?

Rain is so disappointing for miniature goats (they hate that soggy-coat sensation), but sunshine is rejuvenating. You can tell when a goat is savoring those rays. Her ears pitch forward with glee!

Whenever you're feeling a little low, whenever you need that extra **dose of happiness**, consider this ear-forward feeling.

Think about spending time with nature, goat style. Do you have a local park with plenty of trees? Is there a nature reserve in your area where you can take to the trails? If so, goats would likely encourage a visit! (They would also encourage you to eat the rosebushes – but let's not take them up on that last bit of advice!) Still, notice those new scents, those new sights. Explore the wonder of your environment, as you enjoy the sunshine on your hairy coat (um, I mean, your skin!).

When you carve out time for the **wild**, you're also making time for **YOURSELF.**

It's important to note: Happiness isn't a full-time requirement! You can feel a whole range of emotions, even in the space of a single day. But always keep this in mind, young human: **There are bright things ahead.**

Where the
PAWPRINTS LEAD

You see? To understand animals, you don't have to be a person in a fairy tale! You can listen to the creatures in your own yard, in the nature near your home.

They really *are* SPEAKING,
because they're living
in a way that can

INSPIRE US.

At the beginning of this book, I asked you to follow the pawprints and the flipper marks in the sand. And this is where they lead.

TO YOU!

You're unique like the platypus, courageous like the hedgehog, kind like the wombat. You're resilient like Zippy Chippy, confident like Christian, creative like Congo. While you were reading this book, maybe you even heard the animal inside yourself – the one that grows louder the longer you listen. You have all the kindness, all the intelligence, all the individuality.

Everything you need is
already within you!

So, go forth with this knowledge. Remember that you're just like the wonderful animals here, the ones that fly and trot and *thrive*.

NOW, I'D LIKE YOU TO MEET THE FINAL ANIMAL IN THIS BOOK.

Right now, a chimpanzee is knuckle-walking into the room – dragging her fingers against the ground, treading curiously forward. Suddenly, she stops. A mirror blocks her path. She begins to bob her head – back and forth, back and forth – as the hair on her back spikes from fear. *Who is this other chimp? Is she dangerous?* But soon, a look of gleeful recognition sparkles in her eyes. *That's me!* Then she hops, dances, skips across the floor.

Years ago, scientists believed that only humans could recognize themselves in the mirror. But that simply isn't true! It's very clear now: Other animals (like dolphins, elephants, and chimpanzees) can look at their reflections and think, *Whoa, there I am!* It's a moment of surprise – and often delight.

YOU CAN DO THIS, TOO.
YOU CAN DELIGHT IN EVERYTHING THAT YOU ARE!

Instead of looking into the mirror and saying, *Well, I guess that's me,* you could say, *Whoa, there I am! There I am, with all of my wonderful ideas, my friendliness, my bravery. I'm as unique as a platypus! As curious as a raccoon! As openhearted as a capybara!*

This is my best self.

**This is my tail-wagging,
frog-leaping,
lion-hearted self.**

Never be afraid to

ROAR!

Author's Note

The idea for this book arrived as many of my ideas do – while I was out walking my dog, Dany. It occurred to me that Dany (who is wise and generous and kind) might give excellent advice. Then I thought: *What about other animals, like wolves? Like elephants? How might they guide us? What are their lessons?*

So, I started researching. Researching is often my favorite part of any project, but this was extra special. I spent my days poring over stories about animals: articles from *National Geographic* and *Smithsonian Magazine*, scientific studies, the most adorable blog posts from the San Diego Zoo. These stories kept me hopeful, engaged, and comforted in an uncertain time; it is my sincerest wish that they've done the same for you.

I urge you to continue reading about animals – because they're amazing, aren't they? In fact, during my research, I learned so many incredible animal facts, I couldn't squeeze them all into this book. Here are a few of my favorites:

The now-extinct dodo was a member of the pigeon family!

A group of lemurs is called a conspiracy.

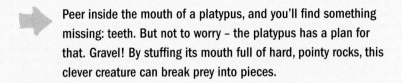 Peer inside the mouth of a platypus, and you'll find something missing: teeth. But not to worry – the platypus has a plan for that. Gravel! By stuffing its mouth full of hard, pointy rocks, this clever creature can break prey into pieces.

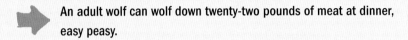 An adult wolf can wolf down twenty-two pounds of meat at dinner, easy peasy.

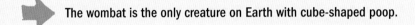 Moles dig separate tunnels for "dining rooms," "kitchens," and "living rooms."

The wombat is the only creature on Earth with cube-shaped poop.

In zebra language, snorting equals happiness; it's basically a laugh!

(A list of full references, for these facts and everything else in this book, is available at *carliesorosiak.com*.)

Finally, since animals give so much to us – like companionship and insight into the natural world – it makes sense to give back to them! If you'd like to help animals in your local community or abroad, the International Fund for Animal Welfare, the ASPCA, and the Best Friends Animal Society are great places to start.

Thanks for listening. The animals say *thank you*, too.

INDEX
OF ANIMALS

Carlie **SOROSIAK**

is the bestselling author of *I, Cosmo*, *My Life As a Cat*, and two novels for young adults. She teaches creative writing at the Savannah College of Art and Design, and lives in Atlanta, Georgia, with her husband and their American dingo.

Katie **WALKER**

is an award-winning illustrator and designer based in sunny Brighton, UK. Katie has had a varied career, working on textile design and children's books, and has also created artwork for a dog-themed board game. Katie loves all things animal, and would love nothing more than to have her own puppy one day soon!